Understanding Foreign Policy

Understanding Foreign Policy

The Foreign Policy Systems Approach

Edited by

Michael Clarke

and

Brian White

Edward Elgar
Cheltenham, UK • Northampton, MA, USA

Published by
Edward Elgar Publishing Limited
Glensanda House
Montpellier Parade
Cheltenham
Glos GL50 1UA
UK

Edward Elgar Publishing, Inc.
136 West Street
Suite 202
Northampton
Massachusetts 01060
USA

Reprinted 1990, 1992, 1994, 1995, 2000, 2002

British Library Cataloguing in Publication Data
Understanding Foreign policy: the foreign policy
systems approach.
1. Foreign relations
I. Clarke, Michael, *1950–* II. White, Brian, *1947–*
327

Library of Congress Cataloguing in Publication Data
Understanding foreign policy: the foreign policy systems
approach/edited by Michael Clarke and Brian White.
p. cm.
Bibliography: p. Includes index.
1. International relations–Research. I. Clarke, Michael,
1950– . II. White, Brian.
JX1291.U46 1989
327'.072—dc20 89–31639
CIP

ISBN 1 85278 123 8 (cased)
1 85278 125 4 (paperback)

Contents

Notes on Contributors

David Allen is Senior Lecturer in Politics, Department of European Studies, Loughborough University.

Michael Clarke is Lecturer in Politics, University of Newcastle upon Tyne.

Christopher Farrands is Senior Lecturer in International Relations, Trent Polytechnic.

Michael Smith is Reader in International Relations, Coventry Polytechnic.

Steve Smith is Senior Lecturer in International Relations, University of East Anglia.

John Vogler is Principal Lecturer in International Relations, Liverpool Polytechnic.

Brian White is Senior Lecturer in International Relations, Staffordshire Polytechnic.

Preface

Understanding Foreign Policy is a new, updated and expanded edition of a book published by the same authors in 1981 under the title, *An Introduction to Foreign Policy Analysis*. The main objective of this new book, however, remains unchanged: to provide students with a readable, accessible introduction to foreign policy analysis. While it does not pretend to summarize the extensive literature in this field, it does offer the would-be analyst a particularly useful way of understanding foreign policy which is based on the notion of a foreign policy system in action. Thus the chapters which follow identify the elements of the foreign policy system, locate the system within its domestic and international context and review the important perspectives on foreign policy behaviour which can be derived from it.

Though these are individual essays they are also collaborative efforts, in that each author commented extensively on the original chapters. While the editors take final responsibility for the content, this book is a genuine group product arising out of several meetings at which draft chapters were discussed and amended. The editors would therefore like to express their thanks to all the contributors.

MICHAEL CLARKE
BRIAN WHITE
March 1988

1. Analysing Foreign Policy: Problems and Approaches

BRIAN WHITE

This book provides an introduction to the study of foreign policy, that area of governmental activity which is concerned with relationships between the state and other actors, particularly other states, in the international system. The chapters which follow develop a useful way of understanding foreign policy that is based on the notion of a foreign policy system: each of these contributions and the overall structure of the book are previewed at the end of this chapter. The main concern here, however, is to introduce some of the basic ideas associated with foreign policy and to highlight the problems posed by foreign policy analysis.

It starts by suggesting that foreign policy itself is important and, therefore, that developing an understanding of foreign policy behaviour is an important activity. Trying to analyse that behaviour, though, presents a number of intellectual challenges which range from defining basic terms to more fundamental methodological problems. Attempts to resolve these problems have led analysts to adopt some simplifying if conventional assumptions about that behaviour. These assumptions collectively have produced what might be called a 'traditional' approach to analysis which has been very influential. Since the 1950s, however, these traditional assumptions have been undermined by the application of a decision-making approach which makes different assumptions about foreign policy behaviour. While this approach in turn has generated a number of problems, it has established what few foreign policy analysts would now dispute, namely that an understanding of the way in which policy is made is central to an understanding of the substance of foreign policy. Certainly the focus on the decision or policy-making process has laid the analytical groundwork for an understanding based on the foreign policy system which is developed in this book.

WHY STUDY FOREIGN POLICY?

The first and most obvious response to this question is to say that scholars and practitioners alike in the field of international relations have an interest in trying to understand what is going on at the international level. Despite important changes in international relations which have broadened the range of actors, the scope of the issues and the complexity of the processes involved, it remains the case that much if not most of what goes on is in fact the product of the foreign policy behaviour of one or more states. Indeed governmental activity in the international sphere has been growing in importance to the extent that states, as agents of welfare as well as warfare, have increased their power, particularly in the period since 1945. At one level at least, international relations consists of an interacting network of foreign policies.

This can be illustrated by reflecting upon international developments in the late 1980s. Commentators are agreed that distinctive changes in East–West relations have occurred which in turn have had a profound impact on the international system as a whole. It is not possible to make sense of these changes, however, without some understanding of the interactions between United States and

Soviet foreign policy. Moreover, given the hostility that characterized East–West relations in the first half of the 1980s, some explanation of specific changes in American and Sovet behaviour is necessary to account for the positive flurry of superpower diplomacy which resulted in the signing of the INF Treaty at the Washington summit in December 1987.

A second related reason for studying foreign policy becomes apparent if we consider the close relationship between this behaviour and crucial issues in international relations that might literally involve life or death on a grand scale. Roy Jones makes this point dramatically: '[Foreign policy] seems to penetrate all that is fundamental to continued human existence and to future human welfare.'[1] The Cuban missile crisis of October 1962 is only the most famous example of an international crisis involving the potential use of nuclear weapons where one mistake by either the United States or the Soviet leadership would have had devastating consequences for the whole international system. An understanding of foreign policy in such a context is almost self-evidently necessary to identify the patterns of behaviour which managed, perhaps fortuitously, to avoid plunging the world into a nuclear war.

Two other important reasons for study emerge from the relationship between foreign policy analysis and the broader study of International Relations. First, foreign policy analysis, with its focus on the state and the ways in which the state relates to the international environment, produces what might be called a 'micro' perspective on international relations. This can be contrasted with a 'macro' perspective which attempts to explain international relations from the level of the international system itself. Explaining international relations from the perspective of the state predisposes the analyst to highlight the differences between states in terms of their foreign policy behaviour and also to take account of the domestic environment of states as a determinant of that behaviour. The sort of explanation of international relations which can be derived from this perspective is distinctly different from that produced by other perspectives which operate at other levels of analysis.[2]

The policy relevance of foreign policy analysis provides another important reason for study. As the branch of International Relations which is most closely connected to government, the findings of academics can, potentially at least, be directly related to governmental policy-making. In some countries indeed, and the United States is a good example, academics are drafted into government on the assumption that their ability to analyse foreign policy behaviour will actually improve the quality of policy-making. There is obviously a possible danger to academic standards of objectivity here, to the extent that analysts might be tempted to offer explanations which they believe government wants to hear. Nevertheless there is a link between the academic study of foreign policy and real world foreign policy-making and this link provides an important reason for study.

ANALYSING FOREIGN POLICY

If the discussion so far has underlined the importance of studying and developing an understanding of foreign policy, we must now turn to what is involved in trying to explain this area of governmental activity by analysing the relevant behaviour. Analysing anything is rather like stripping down an engine, in that it involves the separating out of that which you are trying to explain into its component parts for explanatory purposes. A useful way of thinking about analysis in the context of foreign policy is to see it as providing a necessary framework for posing general 'what', 'why' and 'how' questions. The 'what' here refers to a description of a state's foreign policy. Asking what policy is or has been is obviously important in terms of trying to explain that policy even if description of itself does not provide a very effective explanation. This is partly because description *per se* lends itself to a more or less detailed account of particular foreign policies rather than offering insights into foreign policy behaviour in more general terms. But also, as will become apparent later in this chapter, the 'what' tends to be crucially influenced by the 'why' and the 'how'. Analysis, therefore, must involve going beyond a description of policy past and present to asking why states behave in the way that they do and investigating how foreign policy is made.

Foreign policy analysis starts from the premise that, while there are significant differences between the foreign policies of states, there are enough similar and, therefore, comparable patterns of behaviour to enable the observer to make certain generalized statements about, for example, the goals that states pursue, the range of instruments that they use, who actually makes foreign policy as a result of what influences, and so on. The assumption is that these important 'how' and 'why' questions are answerable by devising appropriate analytical techniques. Foreign policy poses a number of conceptual and empirical problems that the would-be analyst needs to be aware of at the outset, however, and these begin with problems relating to the basic terms 'foreign' and 'policy'.

While a simple definition of foreign policy was offered at the begining of this chapter, it is necessary for the analyst to distinguish 'foreign' policy from other areas of governmental activity. There are two conventional ways of doing this. The first is to treat state frontiers as conceptual as well as territorial boundaries and to separate 'foreign' and 'domestic' policy accordingly. As William Wallace puts it, 'foreign policy is that area of politics which bridges the all-important boundary between the nation-state and its international environment'.[3] Foreign policy, like domestic policy, is formulated within the state, but, unlike domestic policy, is directed at and must be implemented in the environment external to that state. A second way of identifying a specifically 'foreign' area of governmental activity is to assume that this area denotes not only the direction but also a particular type of policy which is concerned with the vital security interests of the state. Because this identifies foreign policy with the most dangerous and sensitive areas of governmental activity, however, some have argued that foreign policy should be shielded from the 'cut and thrust' of domestic political debate. In an important sense, so the argument runs, foreign policy should be apolitical, a point illuminated by the famous aphorism 'politics stops at the water's edge'.

The problem here is that changing patterns of international relations since the Second World War make this rigid differentiation between the state and the international environment difficult to sustain and the separation of 'foreign' and 'domestic' politics look rather arbitrary. An increasing number of governmental activities, particularly in and between advanced industrialized states, are not self-evidently foreign or domestic, either in direction or type. British policies towards the other members of the European Community, for example, cover a wide range of issues. Few of these issues affect British security interests, at least directly, but many if not most of them affect domestic interests as much as 'foreign' policy concerns. Typically, these issues have foreign *and* domestic dimensions and there is often an overlap between the two.

If the meaning of 'foreign' is not always apparent, another set of problems surrounds the term 'policy'. As already noted, foreign policy can simply refer to the external relations of states. Thus, for Joseph Frankel, 'foreign policy consists of decisions and actions which involve to some appreciable extent relations between one state and others'.[4] Some scholars, though, find it more difficult to specify foreign policy. Ralph Pettman, for example, locates foreign policy between 'the grand designs of a De Gaulle, and the day-to-day reactions of diverse policy-makers to foreign events in the light of their habits of response'.[5] This definition may seem unsatisfactorily vague but it does identify two very different conceptions of 'policy' and should alert us to important differences of meaning and connotation. On the one hand, policy is being viewed as an explicit plan of action tailored to serve specific purposes. The West German *Ostpolitik* originally associated with the chancellorship of Willy Brandt would serve as another example. On the other hand, policy can be regarded as a series of habitual responses to events occurring in the international environment. The first conception is activist, the second sees policy as essentially a structured reaction to external stimuli.

Roy Jones offers a rather different but equally instructive conceptual focus by distinguishing between what he calls policy as 'plan or design' and policy as 'practice'. While policy as design, as in Pettman's first usage, is directed towards the attainment of objectives, thereby generating expectations that those objectives will be achieved, Jones reminds us that foreign policy-making is as fallible as the rest of human behaviour: 'It is never free from muddle, from mistaken information, from the clash of personalities, from human infirmity in all its social guises.'[6] Policy as practice, then, refers to a more pragmatic, possibly confused, reaction or adaptation to situations as and when they emerge. Thus 'policy' can denote very different sorts of behaviour.

A third set of problems emerges from the fact that foreign policy presents what William Wallace calls 'boundary' problems. We have already noted that foreign policy crosses the boundary of the state and its international environment. Given that an understanding of foreign policy requires the analyst not only to know something about interactions *between* states but also something about political processes *within* the state, the study of foreign policy also straddles the boundary between two academic disciplines, International Relations and Political Science. The problem here is that each of these disciplines has its own corpus of assumptions, concepts and modes of analysis. Slotting the study of foreign policy into either discipline, therefore, has important implications. If the analyst views foreign policy behaviour from the perspective of International Relations, he or she will be predisposed to see elements of the international environment as the major determinant of foreign policy. A Political Science perspective, on the other hand, predisposes the analyst to highlight domestic determinants like governmental politics, pressure group activity and public opinion. The tendency is for analysis from this perspective to provide a more detailed, perhaps 'messier' picture of foreign policy formulation. This is another dimension of the so-called 'level of analysis' problem that was touched on earlier.[7]

A fourth and final set of difficulties surrounds the acquisition of information about foreign policy. In order to understand and explain this behaviour, it is clearly necessary to collect relevant data. For a variety of reasons, though, the collection of reliable information — hard data as it is often called — can be difficult. First, there can be either too little or too much information available, both of which can create problems for the analyst. To the extent that governments regard foreign policy as a particularly sensitive area of their activities, they may seek to shroud information in secrecy by classifying it or by making it inaccessible in some other way. Britain is a good example of a country which has traditionally had what might be called a 'closed government ethos' and this has created serious problems for scholars trying to investigate governmental behaviour in domestic as well as in foreign policy spheres of activity. More typically, though, analysts are faced not with too little but with too much information that is potentially relevant to an explanation of policy. The problem here is that information taken as evidence may support any number of hypotheses about why a particular state behaved the way it did.

Acquiring information may also be problematic because of what Arnold Wolfers called the 'minds of men' problem.[8] Explaining foreign policy may well require the analyst to, as it were, get 'inside' the minds of policy-makers, to understand their attitudes and beliefs with respect to a particular issue. Indeed the analyst may need to explain the behaviour of those who themselves may have difficulty in explaining why they pursued one course of action rather than another.

This problem is exacerbated by the fact that individual policy-makers and governments collectively are not noted for the frank way in which they comment on policy past and present. Scholars and the wider public tend to get the interpretation of events that the government concerned wants them to have, particularly if that government has anything to hide. Memories have a natural tendency to be selective and the 'facts' can always be selected. The foreign policy analyst must be aware of this problem and endeavour to strip away the reality from the dressing. An excellent example of governmental deception was the 'Belgrano' issue during the Falklands War of 1982. Whether or not the British government was justified in sanctioning the sinking of the Belgrano in the 'fog' of war, it is clear from the evidence of insiders like Clive Ponting that an elaborate deception was worked out to hide the sequence of events which led up to the sinking of the Argentinian cruiser.[9]

If distortion can result from either a paucity or an abundance of relevant information, it can also arise from bias. At it worst, ideological or cultural perspectives can produce crude 'goodies' versus 'baddies' accounts of foreign policy, but there are more subtle ways in which bias can enter into analysis. This can be illustrated by the phenomenon known as ethnocentrism which in this context refers to the placing of a particular country at the centre of world affairs and inflating its importance in the course of world events accordingly. Churchill's influential 'three circles' image where he placed Britain metaphorically at the hub of three interconnected 'circles' of influence is a good example.[10] There is, it should be noted, a bias built into the existing foreign policy literature to the extent that it deals predominantly with the foreign policies of western developed states. While this reflects the origins and interests of most scholars in this field, it does mean that the analytical techniques used may be culture-bound and less than helpful when it comes to explaining the foreign policy behaviour of non-western, less developed states.[11]

This review of the conceptual and empirical problems which confront the foreign policy analyst highlights the need for care in terms of the way in which the task of analysis is undertaken. Indeed it suggests that analysis cannot begin at all until certain choices are made. Specifically, the analyst must decide, either implicitly or explicitly, what unit to base the analysis upon and at what level to pitch the analysis. These basic choices (or assumptions, as they become) are important because they help the analyst to select significant facts and figures from the trivial for attention; but, more importantly, they determine the nature of the ensuing analysis and the sort of explanation produced. Choice of unit identifies the actor or actors whose policy-related behaviour is to be explained: level of analysis determines the perspective from which that behaviour will be explained. These choices in turn are suggestive of particular concepts to be used and questions to be asked.

Collectively, assumptions, concepts and questions constitute an *approach* to analysis, the importance of which has been underlined by Oran Young: 'Everybody views the world in terms of some conceptual framework or approach to analysis [which constitutes] an interrelated set of concepts, variables and assumptions or premises [which] determines what a person regards as worth explaining and what factors he will look for in the search for explanation.'[12] Choosing to explain international politics in terms of the maximization of power, for example, predisposes the analyst to regard as significant data which exemplifies, or can be taken to exemplify, the search for power. It is clearly important then that the assumptions which underpin foreign policy analysis should be made explicit.

TRADITIONAL ANALYSIS AND THE DECISION-MAKING CHALLENGE

One particular approach to the study of foreign policy has been so pervasive over the years that it can be referred to as a 'traditional' approach to foreign policy analysis. One of the attractions of this approach is that it is based upon conventional and straightforward assumptions about foreign policy. We scarcely need to think very hard about any particular example of foreign policy in action to realize that we tend to assume that states have coherent foreign policies which are exemplified by particular actions; that governments have goals or objectives towards which their policies are directed, and that governments calculate not only particular courses of action but also the consequences of that action. We assume, in other words, that foreign policy is the product of rational behaviour; we make what Graham Allison in a very influential study called 'rational actor' assumptions about foreign policy and foreign policy-making.[13]

Joseph Nye has summarized these conventional assumptions which underpin traditional analysis rather more formally under the label of 'state-centric realism'.[14] The state, rather than any other international actor, is regarded as the foreign policy-making unit. More importantly, the state, or rather the government acting on behalf of the state, is treated for analytical purposes as a unitary, monolithic actor; in other words as a collectivity whose behaviour is broadly analogous to that of a purposeful individual.[15] These two assumptions, Nye suggests, are usually harnessed to a Realist analysis which explains state behaviour in terms of an inter-state struggle for power. This serves to reinforce the treatment of the state as a 'billiard ball' interacting with other essentially similar entities. As Realists characterize the international environment as hostile and dangerous, it follows that state behaviour is analysed from the perspective of that environment; forces external rather than internal to the state are regarded as the major determinants of foreign policy. The ability of the state to survive and prosper in such an environment thus provides a focal point for analysis. Survival is seen to hinge around the skilful relating of means to ends, power to purpose.

The most important challenge to these assumptions and the sort of analysis derived from them has come from the application of a decision-making approach to the study of foreign policy. Though the key concepts and assumptions generated by this approach are deceptively simple, it can be argued that the decision-making approach has been more important than any other to the development of foreign policy analysis.[16] There are three central concepts; decision, decision-maker and the decision-making process. The major assumptions which underpin the use of these concepts are as follows. Foreign policy is, in essence, a series of decisions made by a group of people who can be labelled decision-makers. Foreign policy decisions do not simply emerge in response to external stimuli, rather they are processed through an identifiable machinery *within* the state. Broadly, adopting this approach gears foreign policy analysis to the task of explaining the behaviour of an individual or, more typically, a group of people operating within a structured environment who decide (or choose) to pursue one course of action rather than another. Now this decision might relate to foreign policy or to some other type of activity and indeed this approach was applied to other subject areas like Economics, Sociology and Business Administration before it was applied to the study of foreign policy and international relations. The approach was initially applied to foreign policy analysis by Richard Snyder and his associates, who wrote the seminal article in 1954.[17]

In some respects decision-making analysis has reinforced traditional assumptions. Certainly Snyder's 'official decision-makers' appear to act in very much the same way as the purposeful, unitary government of traditional analysis.[18] The notion of an aggregation which acts on behalf of the state is still the dominant conception. To this extent, state-centric assumptions are retained if not reinforced. Decision-making analysts have also tended to reinforce 'rational actor' assumptions by assuming a rational decision-making process. Faced by the question, why does a typical decision-maker choose to pursue one course of action rather than another, analysts have tended to assume that the process begins with a clear objective or set of objectives. The foreign policy decision-maker, like any rational individual, considers possible courses of action and evaluates the likely consequences of each in terms of costs and benefits. The decision-maker then selects the course of action most likely to achieve the desired goal.[19]

There are, of course, good reasons for assuming rational behaviour. In the first place we are predisposed to view man as a rational creature. There is a powerful tradition, certainly in western philosophical thought, of assuming rational purposeful behaviour whenever *homo sapiens* is under the microscope. There is also a second practical reason for assuming rationality. Quite simply, this assumption makes foreign policy-making a lot easier to understand. As Sidney Verba put it: 'if the decision-maker behaves rationally, the observer, knowing the rules of rationality, can rehearse the decisional process in his own mind, and if he knows the decision-makers' goals, can both predict the decision and understand why the particular decision was made'.[20] The task of the analyst then, which might seem overwhelming at first sight given the complexities of foreign policy-making, is greatly simplified by this assumption. It imposes an essential similarity on decision-makers and decision-making, as long as the 'rules' are followed.

A third and final reason for assuming rationality relates to the importance of foreign policy behaviour which was underlined at the beginning of this chapter. It is very comforting to assume that foreign policy decision-makers act rationally, especially when 'life or death' decisions are being contemplated. Indeed some scholars have argued that decision-makers are most likely to behave rationally in crisis situations, when there is considerable pressure upon them to weigh very carefully the consequences of their action. Rational decision-making is certainly a major assumption of the extensive literature on deterrence theory and 'crisis management'.[21] Even if, as other analysts have argued, a rationalistic conception is an imperfect guide to actual foreign policy-making, it remains an important *ideal type* both for scholars and practitioners, providing an important reference point for evaluating the decision-making performance.

The decision-making approach may have reinforced certain aspects of traditional foreign policy analysis, but it has also offered some important challenges to traditional assumptions. In general terms it offers a behavioural rather than a Realist approach to the study. The object of that study is no longer the state which is both abstract and ascribed with human qualities by traditional analysts. Decision-making analysts focus on the behaviour of those who make decisions on behalf of the state. For them the state becomes, by definition, its decision-makers. The fact that decision-makers, unlike abstractions, can be observed (and questioned if they are alive) opens up the possibility that the relevant behaviour can be accurately observed and rigorously analyzed.

More specific challenges are also inherent within the approach. The assumption that foreign policy consists of a series of discrete, identifiable decisions, and therefore that decision-making is the behavioural activity which requires explanation, represents a very different way of approaching the study. Instead of trying to explain state behaviour in terms of its international environment, Snyder suggests that the 'key to the explanation of why the state behaves the way it does lies in the way its decision-makers define their situation'.[22] In other words there is no need to account for the objective 'realities' of the state's environmental situation if the subjective perceptions of decision-makers are what counts. The emphasis on the domestic or internal sources of foreign policy also represents a significant departure from traditional analysis which, as indicated earlier, tends to focus on the impact of external factors on policy. To pursue the billiard ball analogy, traditional analysts have not been predisposed to penetrate the 'hard shell' of the state in order to account for its foreign policy behaviour.

The impact of the decision-making approach can be measured by its impact on the foreign policy literature much of which, since the 1950s, has been geared to the exploration of decision-making assumptions. For example, there have been a number of case studies of specific foreign policy decisions, mainly 'crisis' decisions which may or may not illuminate the way decisions are made in more 'routine' decision-making situations. The notion of the decision-maker's 'definition of the situation' has stimulated a considerable amount of research. The attempt to reconstruct the subjective 'world' of decision-makers has produced research from a foreign policy perspective into a range of psychological and sociological variables that condition and motivate individual and group behaviour. As a result, a number of concepts, research techniques and insights borrowed from Psychology and Sociology have enriched foreign policy analysis. Finally the emphasis on the domestic sources of foreign policy has spawned a number of studies which share the common objective of trying to establish a connection between one or more domestic factors and foreign policy behaviour, such as the nature of the relationship between domestic public opinion and foreign policy.[23]

The most 'subversive' aspect of the decision-making approach as applied to the study of foreign policy, though, has undoubtedly been the focus on the decision-making process. Indeed it can be argued that the most important contribution of the approach has been to instil a general awareness that foreign policy is, to a greater or lesser extent, a product of the way it is made. As James Rosenau observed in the early 1970s:

> For many years, the policy-making process was simply assumed as a necessary prerequisite to the initiation of state action. Today it is commonplace to presume that *what* a state does is in no small way a function of how it decides what to do – in other words, foreign policy action is a product of decisions, and the way decisions are made may substantially affect their contents.[24]

There are, of course, problems with the assumption that all foreign policy behaviour is a product of specific identifiable decisions, as Michael Clarke points out in the next chapter. But the clear implication is that anyone who wants to understand foreign policy must be as concerned with the *making* of policy (the decision or policy process) as they are with the *substance* of that policy.

Analysts have in fact concerned themselves with two related aspects of the foreign policy process; the identity of the policy-making unit and the characteristics of the process. As for the policy-making unit or actor, analysts have broadly adopted either a unitary or a disaggregated conception. While the original Snyder formulation specified the 'official decision-makers' as the policy-making unit whose behaviour is relevant for analytical purposes, analysts have not restricted themselves to investigating the role of 'authoritative' actors in the policy process. As Roger Hilsman noted, 'many more people are involved in the process of government than merely those who hold the duly constituted official positions'.[25] If foreign policy-making is part of a broader domestic political process it will also involve a range of actors – individuals and groups – whose collective behaviour might be distorted by assuming it to be aggregative. This directly challenges the traditional assumption that governments can necessarily be treated as unitary, monolithic foreign policy actors.

In *Essence of Decision* Graham Allison goes as far as to argue that the traditional type of analysis 'must be supplemented, if not supplanted, by frames of reference that focus on the governmental machine – the organizations and the political actors involved in the policy process'.[26] He puts forward two conceptions of the policy process which make different assumptions about, among other things, the actors involved. The first conception, which he calls the 'organizational process model', assumes that for foreign policy purposes 'government consists of a conglomerate of semi-feudal, loosely allied organizations, each with a substantial life of its own'. Thus foreign policy from this perspective is understood to be the product or the 'outputs of large organizations', functioning according to standard patterns of behaviour, 'rather than the deliberate choices of a unified governmental actor'.[27]

Allison's other conception of the policy process also assumes a disaggregated actor, but in this case:

> many actors as players – players who focus not on a single strategic issue, but on many diverse international problems as well; players who act in terms of no consistent set of strategic objectives but rather according to various conceptions of national, organizational and personal goals; players who make governmental decisions not by a single, rational choice but by the pulling and hauling that is politics.[28]

Instead of the traditional hard distinction between foreign and domestic politics, this 'governmental or bureaucratic politics model' assumes that the foreign policy-making process shares many of the characteristics of domestic policy formation. Accordingly foreign policy is conceived from this perspective not as governmental choice or as organizational output, but as the outcome or 'resultant' of various bargaining games among the key players within the government.

Clearly assumptions made about the nature of the policy-making unit affect the way that the policy process is characterized. It is difficult, for example, to assume a rational policy process if a unified actor cannot be assumed. Several analysts have in fact undermined 'rational actor' assumptions by arguing that a rational model is a poor guide to actual foreign policy decision-making, particularly in an organizational context. They argue that such assumptions are unrealistic because decision-makers rarely have sufficient time or information to follow through this sort of process. On the basis of observing the decision-making process in large organizations, Herbert Simon coined the term 'bounded rationality' to incorporate the constraints on decision-makers and suggested that the principle of 'satisficing' rather than 'optimizing' more realistically characterizes the process.[29] What this means is that in practice the decision-maker will only search for alternative courses of action until one is found which meets certain minimum (usually organizationally defined) criteria. This is closely related to the distinctly non-rational notion of decision-making referred to less than politely by Charles Lindblom as 'muddling through'.[30]

THE FOREIGN POLICY SYSTEM

If analysts find it difficult to agree on ways of characterizing the foreign policy process, as the last section has indicated, few of them would disagree with the proposition that an understanding of that process is crucial to an understanding of foreign policy. The complexities of that process particularly in advanced industrialized states, however, make analysis inherently difficult. In order to capture the dynamics of the various types of behaviour involved, many analysts have found it useful to think about the process of producing foreign policy as if it was a more or less complex system of action. This is the starting point of the approach to an understanding of foreign policy that is offered in this book.

Chapter 2 shows how the system approach can serve as a framework for analysis, an organizing device which is sufficiently broad and flexible to encompass the major processes and interactions involved in producing foreign policy. The system approach cannot of itself explain foreign policy but it does help the analyst to construct explanations by setting out the range of variables involved and the possible interrelationships between them. This chapter applies the system analogy to a foreign policy context and identifies in some detail the relevant components of a foreign policy system. It also considers some of the uses of the system approach and the sorts of assumptions which need to be made in order to make appropriate use of it.

A foreign policy system, like any other system, does not operate in a vacuum. The behaviour or, to use systems language, the 'outputs' generated by the system are conditioned by influences which operate outside the boundaries of the system, but which can and do serve as significant 'inputs' into the foreign policy system. The next two chapters discuss a number of different contextual or environmental factors which condition foreign policy behaviour. From a system perspective they are seen to motivate, modify, constrain or in some other way affect the workings and the operation of the foreign policy system. One simple way of thinking about these environmental factors is to see them as a collection of demands and constraints which have an impact on foreign policy. Some of these factors can be located conveniently in the domestic environment of the state, and some in the international environment that is common to all states. But some, such as economic processes, cross the boundary between the state and its international environment.

Most of the factors dealt with in Chapter 3 can be located in the external environment of states though there are important processes that characterize the contemporary environment, such as transnationalism and transgovernmentalism, which transcend state frontiers. Elements within the international environment, it is argued in this chapter, serve as particularly significant inputs into the foreign policy system because all states exist within that environment and it is extremely difficult, even for the most powerful states, to isolate themselves from the ubiquitous structures and processes and the global scope of the contemporary international system.

Chapter 4 also discusses the influence of the international environment, but focuses on other contextual factors which impact on the policy process, such as social structure and culture, physical and economic environments and what is referred to as the 'knowledge structure'. An important theme which runs through both these chapters but which is dealt with in some detail here, is the 'free will versus determinism' debate. To what extent does the environment determine policy? To what extent do foreign policy-makers have real choices? While it is accepted that structures both internal and external to the state can and do shape policy, a crude determinism is rejected here and this chapter concludes by setting up a useful framework for analysing the relationship between the environment and the policy process.

Having explained the system approach and set the foreign policy system in context, the second half of this book focuses on what are regarded as the most important types of explanation of foreign policy that can be derived from the system framework. Specifically, three sets of approaches are considered which are important because they provide different perspectives on how the foreign policy system operates and because, in different ways, they challenge the traditional 'unitary-rational' account of the policy process. A fourth perspective dealt with here is less a type of explanation and more a broad comparative framework for analysis which draws together much of the material considered in the first three.

Chapter 5 deals with the bureaucratic politics perspective. The starting point here is the influential work of

Graham Allison and, in particular, Allison's alternative models of the policy process which were outlined earlier in this chapter. Allison's work is important because it has stimulated over the last twenty years or so a considerable amount of research on the impact of bureaucratic actors and organizational structures on the foreign policy process. The development of this research perspective, however, has been punctuated by a welter of critical reviews, at both empirical and methodological levels, many of them directed at Allison's orginal work on the Cuban missile crisis. This chapter discusses in some detail the problems that have been identified but, by following the debate into the 1980s, it is also able to chart the positive contribution of Allison's work and, more broadly, the contribution of the bureaucratic politics perspective to developing our understanding of how foreign policy systems work.

Chapter 6 introduces a second perspective which encompasses the contribution of various psychological approaches and theories to an understanding of foreign policy behaviour. As noted earlier, the idea that the decision-makers' 'definition of the situation' is crucial to an explanation of their decision-making behaviour has generated a great deal of research which attempts to construct the subjective 'world' of individual or groups of foreign policy decision-makers in different situations. This chapter looks at approaches which attempt to describe the psychological environment of decision-makers and, more significantly perhaps in foreign policy terms, it also offers an evaluation of theories which purport to explain faulty decision-making and the problem of misperception in particular. A third section reviews the findings of research which has focused on a specific 'situational variable' – namely the psychological aspects of decision-making in a crisis. The general conclusion is that research in this area has provided a number of striking insights into foreign policy behaviour, particularly with respect to the constraints that may be imposed on decision-makers by the operation of cognitive processes. This perspective, however, should not be seen in isolation, but rather in terms of possible interrelationships with other perspectives such as bureaucratic politics.

A third perspective which focuses on problems of implementing foreign policy is discussed in Chapter 7. This perspective, it can be argued, is distinctive in two related ways. First, bureaucratic politics and cognitive approaches are good examples of established perspectives which have attracted a considerable amount of research that is well documented in the literature. Students of foreign policy, however, have only relatively recently discovered the importance of implementation as a perspective and there is not as yet an extensive literature in foreign policy analysis, though this is not true of other areas of policy analysis.[31] This can be explained in part at least by the fact that most research efforts in this field have been geared to explaining how and why decisions are *made*. To this extent the decision-making approach has had a restricting influence on the development of foreign policy analysis. A concern with the problems of *implementing* decisions has been assumed to be peripheral at best to the central task of explaining the making of decisions. Work on organizational behaviour in particular, however, has led some scholars to realize that a consideration of problems which emerge at the implementation 'stage' of the policy process throws a considerable amount of light on how the foreign policy system works *as a whole*. Indeed, as Chapter 7 illustrates, it is already clear from the limited amount of work done which has adopted this perspective that much of the dynamism of the policy process is lost by seeing it essentially in policy-making terms.[32]

The perspectives dealt with in this book are not, of course, the only explanatory perspectives that can be derived from the system framework, but it can be argued that they are the most useful in terms of developing an understanding of foreign policy. Both to appreciate their merits and to put them into some sort of analytical context, it is worth noting here that there are broadly three types of explanation which can be derived from the system approach. The first type operates at the level of the international system and regards the foreign policy system as a subsystem of the international system. Theories which operate at this level see foreign policy as the response of that subsystem to the structure of the international system.[33] Strictly, these are general system theories rather than perspectives derived from the foreign policy system, but they do offer descriptions, explanations and predictions about foreign policy behaviour. The problem with this group of 'macro' theories is that they are designed to offer explanations of the workings of the international system rather than an account of state behaviour *per se*, which tends as a result to be explained in very general and abstract terms only. Moreover, because these theories tend to regard the foreign policy system as a dependent subsystem of the international system, their explanation of foreign policy also tends to be deterministic. For these writers the nature of the international system rather than the foreign policy system determines the nature of foreign policy.

A second type of explanation attempts to explain foreign policy at the level of the foreign policy system. This group of theories can be described as 'input–output' because their prime concern is to relate the 'output' of the system – foreign policy behaviour – to the 'inputs' to that system from both the domestic and external environments of the state.[34] The processes through which these inputs must pass in order to be converted into outputs, however, are treated for analytical purposes as a 'black box', into which stimuli flow and responses somehow emerge. The fact that these theories tend to ignore the policy process which, it might be argued, is central to the operation of the whole system, serves to limit their utility.

The perspectives dealt with in this book can be located within a third set of approaches which use the foreign policy system as a framework for research. What these approaches have in common is their concern to develop an understanding of how the system as a whole, and the policy process in particular, works. Each perspective offers different sorts of insights into the operation of the system, whether by focusing on organizational behaviour and bureaucratic politics, cognitive processes or problems of implementation. By focusing attention on particular aspects or characteristics of the policy process, each perspective can consider a relatively small number of variables, and can thus deal effectively with manageable; researchable questions and issues. This work, it can be argued, constitutes a useful exercise in partial theory building, contributing to an understanding of how the foreign policy system works in a gradual or piecemeal way.

Much of the research undertaken, as detailed in the relevant chapters, is concerned to develop or refine approaches within a particular perspective. A natural extension of the perspectives approach, however, is to see how different perspectives interconnect. Some interesting research has taken these perspectives themselves as 'building blocks', using the system framework to consider possible interrelationships between different perspectives. John Steinbruner, for example, has developed what he calls a cybernetic model of foreign policy-making in which he combines bureaucratic and cognitive perspectives in order to capture the central dynamics of the policy process.[35] Perhaps the most ambitious research project undertaken to date which attempts to interrelate the insights provided by several different perspectives is the complex system model developed by Michael Brecher and his research associates and applied to an analysis of Israeli foreign policy.[36] This work is based on a major research design outlined by Brecher, Steinberg and Stein in 1969.[37] This design mapped out the key elements of the system and offered clear guidelines on how to carry out research utilizing its concepts and categories. The Brecher project has produced some interesting studies, but it has also illustrated the limits of the more ambitious system model. The amount of empirical material needed to 'operationalize' the research design is vast, and it is not at all clear that the insights into foreign policy behaviour that have been generated are such as to justify the expenditure in research time and effort.

Nevertheless Brecher's work, which explicitly deploys a comparative perspective both with respect to a particular country — Israel — and in his later project on crisis decision-making, with respect to particular cases, provides a convenient link to the final chapter in this book. Chapter 8 moves away from specific perspectives to consider the general insights into foreign policy behaviour that can be derived from the system approach. As noted earlier in this introductory chapter, one of the main objectives of foreign policy analysis is to develop comparative analyses of behaviour. Chapter 8 draws together many of the themes and perspectives discussed in other chapters and uses them to develop a comparative framework for analysis which can be applied to particular cases and issues. In order to make sense of what follows, however, the reader must start with some understanding of the notion of the foreign policy system and this is taken up in the next chapter.

NOTES

[1] Jones, R. E., *Analysing Foreign Policy*, London, Routledge & Kegan Paul, 1970, p. 11.
[2] Singer, J. D., 'The Level of Analysis Problem in International Relations' in Knorr, K. and Verba, S., eds, *The International System: Theoretical Essays*, Princeton, NJ, Princeton University Press, 1961, pp. 77–92. This classic essay sets the 'problem' within the more general context of International Relations.
[3] Wallace, W., *Foreign Policy and the Political Process*, London, Macmillan, 1971, p. 7.
[4] Frankel, J., *The Making of Foreign Policy*, London, Oxford University Press, 1963, p. 1.
[5] Pettman, R., *Human Behaviour and World Politics*, London, Macmillan, 1975, p. 41.
[6] Jones, R. E., op. cit. p. 11.
[7] James Rosenau argues that this boundary-crossing characteristic of foreign policy requires the setting up of a separate study which he calls 'linkage politics'. See Rosenau, J. N., *Linkage Politics*, New York, Free Press, 1969.
[8] Wolfers, A., *Discord and Collaboration*, Baltimore, Johns Hopkins University Press, 1962, pp. 4ff.
[9] Ponting, C., *The Right to Know*, London, Sphere, 1985, Part 2.

[10] This image was first presented in a speech to the Conservative Party Conference in 1948.
[11] For an interesting attempt to analyse the foreign policy behaviour of Third World states, see Calvert, P., *The Foreign Policy of New States*, Brighton, Wheatsheaf, 1986.
[12] Young, O. R., 'The Perils of Odysseus: On Constructing Theories in International Relations', in Tanter, R. and Ullman, R. H., eds, *Theory and Policy in International Relations*, Princeton, NJ, Princeton University Press, 1972, p. 188.
[13] Allison, G. T., *Essence of Decision: Explaining the Cuban Missile Crisis*, Boston, Little, Brown, 1971.
[14] Nye, J. S. in Goodwin, G. L. and Linklater, A., eds, *New Dimensions in World Politics*, London, Croom Helm, 1975, p. 36.
[15] Some writers encompass both these assumptions by employing a 'state-as-billiard-ball' analogy. See, for example, Wolfers, A., op. cit. pp. 19ff.
[16] For a more developed attempt to evaluate the impact of a decision-making approach on the study of foreign policy, see White, B. P., 'Decision-making Analysis' in Taylor, T., ed., *Approaches and Theory in International Relations*, London, Longman, 1978, pp. 141–64.
[17] Snyder, R. C., Bruck, H. W. and Sapin, B., 'Decision-making as an Approach to the Study of International Politics', reprinted in Snyder, R. C. *et al.*, *Foreign Policy Decision-Making: An Approach to the Study of International Politics*, New York, Free Press, 1962.
[18] ibid. p. 99.
[19] See the 'rational actor' model or 'Model 1' in Allison, G. T., op. cit. pp. 10–38.
[20] Verba, S., 'Assumptions of Rationality and Non-Rationality in Models of the International System' in Rosenau, J. N., ed., *International Politics and Foreign Policy*, New York, Free Press, 1969, p. 225.
[21] Morgan, P. M., *Deterrence: A Conceptual Analysis*, Beverley Hills, Calif., Sage, 1977; and Williams, P., *Crisis Management*, London, Martin Robertson, 1975, are good examples of this literature.
[22] Snyder, R. C. *et al.*, op. cit. p. 65.
[23] See, for example, Cohen, B., *The Public's Impact on Foreign Policy*, Boston, Little, Brown, 1973.
[24] Rosenau, J. N., ed., op. cit. p. 169.

[25] Hilsman, R. in ibid. p. 235.
[26] Allison, G. T., op. cit. p. 5.
[27] ibid. p. 67.
[28] ibid. p. 144.
[29] Simon, H. A., *Administrative Behaviour*, New York, Macmillan, 1959; see also McGrew, A. G. and Wilson, M. J., eds, *Decision-Making: Approaches and Analysis*, Manchester, Manchester University Press, 1982, Section 2.
[30] Lindblom, C. E., 'The Science of "Muddling Through"', *Public Administration Review*, 19, 1959, pp. 79–99; id., 'Still Muddling, Not Yet Through', in McGrew, A. G. and Wilson, M. J., eds, op. cit. pp. 125–38.
[31] For examples, see the references in the notes attached to Chapter 7.
[32] See also Smith, S. and Clarke, M., eds, *Foreign Policy Implementation*, London, Allen & Unwin, 1985.
[33] See, for example, Kaplan, M. A., *System and Process in International Politics*, New York, Wiley, 1964; Rosecrance, R., *Action and Reaction in World Politics*, Boston, Little, Brown, 1963; and *International Relations: Peace or War?* New York, McGraw-Hill, 1973.
[34] See, for example, Rosenau, J. N., *The Study of Political Adaptation*, London, Pinter, 1981; Hanrieder, W., 'Compatibility and Consensus: A Proposal for the Conceptual Linkage of External and Internal Dimensions of Foreign Policy' in Hanrieder, W., ed., *Comparative Foreign Policy: Theoretical Essays*, New York, McKay, 1971, pp. 242–64.
[35] Steinbruner, J. D., *The Cybernetic Theory of Decision*, Princeton, NJ, Princeton University Press, 1975.
[36] This model is shown diagrammatically on p. 32. For Brecher's work on Israel, see Brecher, M., *The Foreign Policy System of Israel*, Oxford, Oxford University Press, 1972; and *Decisions in Israel's Foreign Policy*, Oxford, Oxford University Press, 1974.
[37] Brecher, M., Steinberg, B. and Stein, J., 'A Framework for Research on Foreign Policy Behaviour', *Journal of Conflict Resolution*, 13, 1, 1969, pp. 75–101.

2. The Foreign Policy System: A Framework for Analysis

MICHAEL CLARKE

It is clear from the first chapter that the study of foreign policy decision-making is far from straightforward. Indeed, even the term 'decision-making' may be misleading, since it implies that foreign policy can be broken down into a series of observable decisions: conscious choices as in some sort of game of political chess. But any study of a state's foreign policy over a given period quickly reveals that rather than a series of clear decisions, there is a continuing and confusing 'flow of action', made up of a mixture of political decisions, non-political decisions, bureaucratic procedures, continuations of previous policy, and sheer accident. For both practitioners and observers, the reality of policy-making is extremely messy. The most eloquent and challenging expression of this insight is probably to be found in Tolstoy's *War and Peace*. For Tolstoy did not believe that political leaders are the shapers of history; they merely have to fit into the 'course of events', which in reality are driven by more anonymous forces. 'We say: Napoleon chose to invade Russia and he did so. In reality we never find in all Napoleon's career anything resembling an expression of that design.'[1] Even generals conducting their battles, he said, 'of all the blind instruments of history were the most enslaved and involuntary'.[2] Whether or not we would agree with Tolstoy, he is alerting his readers to the fact that in hindsight policies are made to appear more deliberate and consistent than they ever were at the time. For the practitioner struggling with an immediate political issue, there is a tide of events into which they must attempt to inject comprehension, order and, on occasion, some political direction.

Though we know this to be the reality, this does not mean that the concept of decision-making is meaningless. Rather, we should realize that the idea of decision-making does not refer only to the making of conscious choices, but also to a range of personal, organizational, institutional and environmental factors which also help account for the flow of events. Not all that goes on in the realm of decision-making is actually decision — in the sense of being a single human choice — and we must find some way in which to characterize the range and depth of that political activity which produces foreign policy action.

To do this, students of foreign policy have employed the main principles of systems analysis to examine the activities involved in the decision-making process. This involves viewing foreign policy as if it were a system.[3] In reality we know that human behaviour and organizations do not actually exist as a system: only organisms and machines are tangible systems in operation. But we can view any set of human routines as if they were a system, as a way of organizing our thoughts about them. In other words we can begin to describe the complex business of foreign policy by using the metaphor of a system. A foreign policy system will have inputs, processes and outputs; like any machine or organism there is some sort of fuel or stimuli at one end, a process which responds to such inputs to transform them or react to the them, and an end product of some description which constitutes the performance of the system. For the basic metaphor to be complete, it is also necessary to note that any system must be conceived as operating in an environment; a set of circumstances which partly determines the operation and

Figure 2.1 **The Basic Political System**

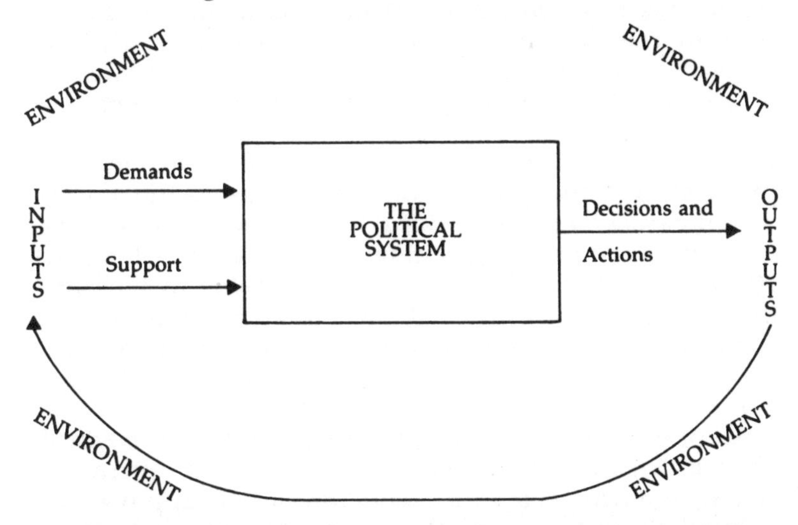

Reprinted from Easton, D. *A Framework for Political Analysis.* Prentice-Hall Inc., 1965, p. 112, by permission of the publishers.

existence of the system. The output of any system, therefore, inevitably goes into the environment of it and that, in turn, will have some effect on the way the system subsequently works. This is known by the inelegant name of 'feedback' or even a 'feedback loop', where outputs go into the environment to become more inputs to which the system must respond. The bare bones of this sort of conception, as presented originally by David Easton, are set out in *Figure 2.1*.

Easton's work in the late 1950s and that of other political scientists of the same generation, created turmoil in the study of politics, as they elevated the metaphor of a system to become the basis of an ambitious theory of political science in general.[4] According to systems theorists, *anything* in political science can be seen as a system and analysed according to its inputs and outputs. Such inputs and outputs are made up of patterns of behaviour, though we sometimes find such patterns difficult to recognize. But the system could only be affected by tangible actions. Rules and constitutions, attitudes and aspirations were only relevant in so far as they could be seen to translate into a pattern of behaviour. So the analyst's task was first, to define whatever system was to be studied; a government, a foreign policy, a region, a local council, a process of democratization, a company or whatever. Second, it was necessary to define what inputs, processes and outputs could be regarded as essential parts of that particular system. Third, because inputs, processes and outputs could only be things which had some tangible effect, so in principle it should be possible to measure them. Thus having defined their systems, analysts set about trying to define and measure their components and collect data on those patterns of observable human behaviour which would have a system effect.

All of this created something of a revolution in political science; for systems analysis became, almost overnight and with all the zeal of a revolution, a new approach to political study. The metaphor of the system had become not only a theory of political action but also a new methodology for the study of such action. To its proponents it was scientific method applied to real political phenomena. To its opponents it was quantitative analysis or 'number-crunching' for its own sake in a way that ignored the importance of abstractions and ideas in political life.[5] Fortunately it is not necessary to take sides on such issues to pursue a foreign policy systems approach. Though the systems analysis approach has failed to revolutionize the study of international politics, it has nevertheless left us with a well-developed awareness of how to use at least the metaphor of a system as a way of organizing our thoughts and achieving greater understanding of the phenomena that make up foreign policy analysis. We do not need to be systems theorists in our outlook, or behaviouralists in our methodology, to articulate a useful foreign policy system.

An impressive attempt to do this over many years has been made by Michael Brecher in relation to Israeli foreign policy. In 1972 he set out a basic 'research design' of a system of Israeli foreign policy which he has since attempted to utilize.[6] The outline is presented in *Figure 2.2.* It is a reasonably complex design and while it is not our intention to follow it through, its essential features do illustrate a number of characteristics which apply to all such designs. First, the attempt to formulate a foreign policy system compels one to specify the components of it. We have to think through how we can characterize the forces which matter, what differentiates them from other forces, and where in the system they should most appropriately be placed. In other words, in order to produce a useful simplification of variables, it is necessary first to produce an acceptable specification of them. Second, the system must be conceived as a whole; that is the rationale for having it outlined on one sheet of paper. To appreciate its systemic qualities it is necessary to have all of it in view, even though our understanding of some parts of it will be much better than others. Third, though this representation of it is static, the conception behind the foreign policy system is, of necessity, dynamic. We are trying to capture the essence of a system of human action so we are trying to describe a continuous process; to encompass on paper the idea that it is constantly in operation, reacting to stimuli, changing and adapting. Fourth, it is always necessary to see the system in relation to its environment, however one chooses to specify it. The system cannot but be affected by the forces surrounding it. Finally the components of the system, the variables, are obviously interdependent and so will react continuously with each other. Some, such as environmental factors, will be more independent than others, but all will be systemically related.

Any articulation of a foreign policy system will have these general characteristics. Without going to the extent of examining all of the detail of Brecher's research design, we can nevertheless easily specify some of the major variables that are suggested in Easton's basic outline in *Figure 2.1*, to construct a foreign policy system. Inputs and outputs are the easier forces to specify. Inputs consist of all internal and external forces which bear in on decision-makers. The most notable inputs are usually perceived as

Figure 2.2 **Brecher's 'Research Design' for the Study of Israeli Foreign Policy**

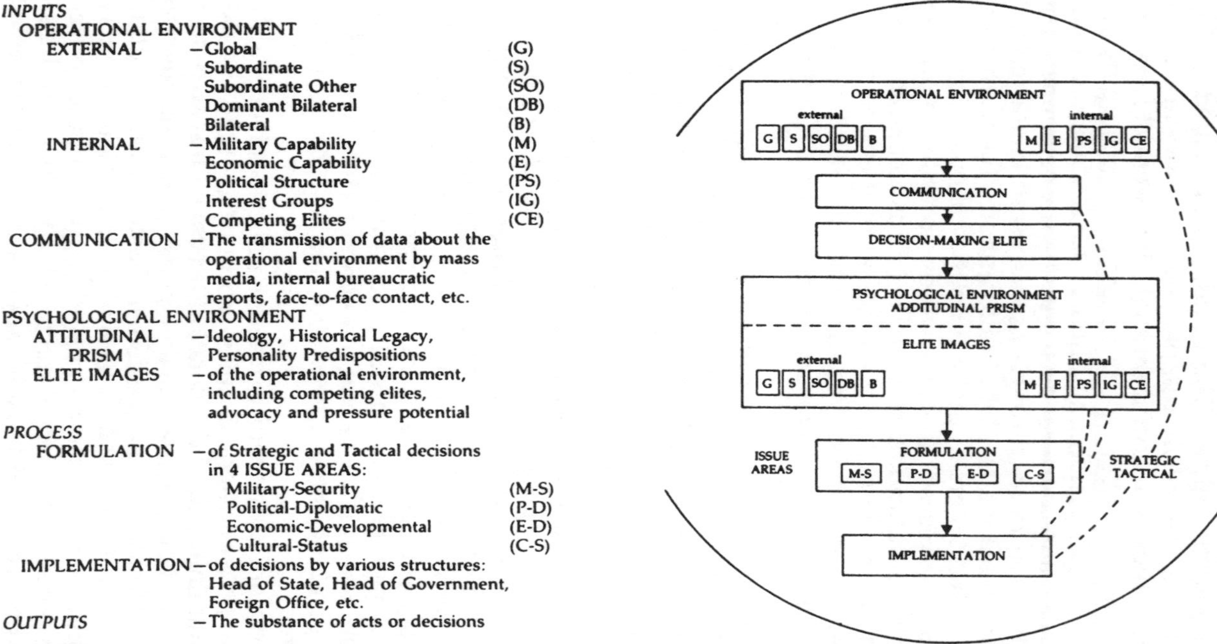

INPUTS
OPERATIONAL ENVIRONMENT
EXTERNAL —Global (G)
Subordinate (S)
Subordinate Other (SO)
Dominant Bilateral (DB)
Bilateral (B)
INTERNAL —Military Capability (M)
Economic Capability (E)
Political Structure (PS)
Interest Groups (IG)
Competing Elites (CE)
COMMUNICATION —The transmission of data about the operational environment by mass media, internal bureaucratic reports, face-to-face contact, etc.
PSYCHOLOGICAL ENVIRONMENT
ATTITUDINAL PRISM —Ideology, Historical Legacy, Personality Predispositions
ELITE IMAGES —of the operational environment, including competing elites, advocacy and pressure potential
PROCESS
FORMULATION —of Strategic and Tactical decisions in 4 ISSUE AREAS:
Military-Security (M-S)
Political-Diplomatic (P-D)
Economic-Developmental (E-D)
Cultural-Status (C-S)
IMPLEMENTATION—of decisions by various structures: Head of State, Head of Government, Foreign Office, etc.
OUTPUTS —The substance of acts or decisions

Reprinted from Brecher. M., *The Foreign Policy System of Israel.* Oxford University Press, 1972, pp. 3–4, by permission of the publishers.

pressures. There may be external pressures from allies to increase defence expenditure on expensive weapons systems that are jointly produced; and internal pressure not to do so from domestic weapons producers who face a loss of business, or perhaps from the legislators who perceive a loss of sovereignty. Internal and external pressures may run in the same direction, perhaps to reduce interest rates or to expand the economy. In the contemporary world of the developed states, internal and external pressures tend increasingly to feed off each other as economic interests overlap state boundaries and as communication and the forces of interdependence conspire to internationalize political problems. Inputs, however, are not only pressures and demands, and they are not at all internally consistent. More subtly, inputs can be conceived of as supports and reinforcements to decision-makers; not only expressions of political support from allies and party interests, but also less tangible factors such as the power of tradition or the perception of continuity provided by a vigorous constitution. Inputs, therefore, are not simply issues, but also any salient forces which are not themselves part of the decision-making process but which can be seen as having an effect upon it.

At the other end of the machine are the outputs of policy. These are easily confused because the literature of international politics and foreign policy has not dealt with them particularly clearly. It is commonplace in many traditional textbooks to define the actions of states in the world as a mixture of techniques on a spectrum ranging from war and conflict at one end, through a list of less unpleasant pressures, towards the diplomacy of pure persuasion at the other.[7] This is indeed a useful conception of techniques of state action. But it is not a good description of the policy output itself; for the machine does not produce 'war' or 'economic pressure' or 'diplomacy'. These are gross characterizations of the outcome in international relations of the interaction between different foreign policies. As such, they are international phenomena. Real outputs are much more specific and consist of a great body of statements, declarations, orders, contacts, conversations, publicity handouts, visits, replies to letters, and so on *ad infinitum*. If we wish to bring some order to this variety of activity we might define outputs as falling into five or six different types. One type is 'informational' where the process simply aims to disseminate information and perhaps policy rationales, as in the publication of annual statements on defence. Another would be 'declaratory' where decision-makers want to take a political stance on something. A great deal of the output of a foreign policy system is of this type. A third type we might call 'procedural' or 'functional' where action is designed to facilitate something else; to set up meetings and conferences, to coordinate negotiating drafts, to communicate in order to facilitate the actions of a domestic agency, and so on. Another type is the output of goods and services or the administration of transfer payments. These derive from the traditionally domestic functions of government, where it is expected to produce something or, as in the tax system, to manage the transfer of money from one group to another. Surprisingly little of the output of foreign policy involves such activities, except for the case of defence which is a prime example of the processes of creating goods and services and handling transfer payments. Defence, however, is intimately involved with the domestic economy, and though foreign and domestic policies are becoming more mixed, in essence foreign policy is not dominated by physical production or high expenditure. A final sort of output might be classed as overt or physical action; where leaders must attend summits, or military activity must take place. Such activity is not necessarily a prelude to conflict or war: it may perhaps be for the purposes of disaster relief or as a measure of prudence in a deteriorating situation. Other categories can be imagined, but this list offers a flavour of the diversity that is inherent in foreign policy outputs.

Between inputs and outputs, we have to attempt to specify 'processes'. Of course, in any human system there are no end of factors that could be included, and the complexity of even the most simple decision processes is infinite. Nevertheless a model of politics is no use unless it does simplify the complexity of the real world, and in this case it is possible to offer some broad characterizations of the processes which normally occur within the 'black box' at the centre of the decison-making system. To begin with, all inputs have to be interpreted. They are meaningless until they are translated into facts that are perceived to be relevant by the officials and politicians who work within the system. It is entirely possible for inputs to be over– or undervalued because of the way in which the system interprets them. In the 1950s, for example, the British government did not respond coherently to the economic and political pressures which urged it to join in the foundation of a European Community, not least because the governmental process did not know how to interpret pressures as diverse as those which led other governments to embrace such an innovative idea. In the United States, by contrast, the Jewish lobby is often seen as an important input to the policy process which is overvalued in the way it is seen to affect such a wide range of issues. American policy-makers, it is sometimes claimed, give the lobby undue weight.

Once interpreted, inputs have to be compounded into 'issues' which make some political sense to the decision-maker, and then communicated around the system. The British Foreign Office, for example, has a 'crisis room' at the top of its main building which is manned by whoever the appropriate officials may be in a particular crisis. All communication is then routed to and from it so as to ensure that vital information is not locked up somewhere else in the system by routines that apply in normal circumstances.[8] Clearly the aggregation of inputs into comprehensible issues and the communication of them throughout the system will be a function of both the bureaucratic structure of the system and the psychology of politicians and officials. In this respect structure and psychology constantly interact to provide standard operating procedures, or rules, as well as characteristic operating procedures, or norms, with which issues are handled. As issues make their way through the machinery, gathering other issues which have some bearing on them, being filtered and adapted, and made to fit into the perspective of those dealing with them, so some issues will be brought to the point of political choice. In some cases there will be a perception that a choice between alternatives will have to be made. It may be made in any number of ways; by one person alone, by a committee, in a single meeting, or gradually through a series of meetings where alternatives are steadily narrowed down, or perhaps in a mixture of fora which independently tend towards the same conclusions. Other issues, however, will not be elevated to the point of a conscious political choice. Decisions on such issues are, in effect, still made, since to do nothing is a way of handling a problem and consequences will flow from that 'masterly inactivity', as it is known among bureaucrats. In other words, for very many issues alternatives are not consciously articulated even though in principle they always exist. Instead the decision process merely monitors the issue as it passes through and deals with it as a routine output. Between these two extremes many variations are possible in the degree of conscious choice accorded to any particular issue. Action will flow from all of them. At one extreme the action is unique, at the other it is pure routine. Most issues provoke a response that is a mixture of routines, though the precise mixture of them is unique to that issue.

Finally it is necessary to specify the nature of the environment in which the system exists. In many respects this would be an impossible task since the number of relevant variables would simply defy comprehension. In reality, however, analysts do not normally try to specify its general components. Instead it is sufficient to be aware that environmental factors matter, and then to construct the relevant elements of it for the given issue under consideration. If the policy under discussion is a western defence policy, for instance, then the most relevant components in the environment are likely to be NATO, other allies, international defence interests, domestic defence interests, the reaction of adversarial states or alliances, and so on. For a different type of issue, a separate constellation of forces would be regarded as relevant.

All of this offers us some idea of how to specify the foreign policy system so that the metaphor is developed. In order to use it to aid our understanding, however, it is necessary to appreciate both its uses and its limitations.

THE USES OF FOREIGN POLICY SYSTEMS

The most obvious use of the systems approach should be clear from the previous section. The system is an organizing device that forces us to specify the relevant variables and establish the boundaries between them. It also forces us to take a view, in the way that we arrange the components, of how we think the process might work. In this respect the formulation is also behavioural. This does not mean that it is necessary to accept behaviouralist methodology, but rather that it is necessary to realize that the components of the system are defined by their functions within the system rather than by their formal institutions, or their political or constitutional authority. Traditional accounts of British foreign policy, for instance, which only outline the functions of decision-makers according to their official role and the institution of government to which they belong, can at best tell only part of the story. Constitutional functions and official boundaries are obviously important but actual patterns of behaviour, influence and communication will always cross institutional boundaries.

According to the 'constitution' of Britain, for instance, the House of Commons performs its function of scrutinizing the foreign policy of the government through debates and Question Time. But all students of foreign policy in Britain know that such channels are highly ineffective and that real scrutiny, in so far as it can be exercised by parliamentarians, is a much less formal, interpersonal process that works partly through Select Committees, but mainly through channels of intra-party dialogue. The Commons does, on the other hand, perform a more effective function in acting as a vocal channel of concern on certain emotive and well-publicized issues that successive governments would have preferred to ignore, such as British trade with South Africa or the treatment of Jews and dissidents in the Soviet Union. In this respect the Commons provides a relevant input to the foreign policy system through the function that it performs, in practice more effectively. We must also remember that informal policy processes change more easily over time as personalities and habits change. The behaviour of Congress in relation to United States foreign policy, for example, has altered dramatically since the early 1970s and is liable to change with every new influx of politicians to Capitol Hill and the White House. The system approach, therefore, seeks to organize the material widely enough to include both formal and informal aspects, and makes explicit the unlimited number of physical and psychological operations involved in making the process work.

A second use of the system approach is that it allows us to say something about the general activity of foreign policy, not just to characterize the machinery of one state. We can therefore treat foreign policy both as an activity of the state and as a phenomenon of world politics. Foreign policies have similar demands made upon them and exist in an international system which affects them all. There are obviously great variations between different foreign policies. But if they were entirely discrete then the web of diplomacy and a great deal of what we know takes place in the international system would be impossible. Foreign policy is understood as a function of government and also as part of the international system. We can use a system approach to organize our thoughts on foreign policy at both levels.

Third, and related to this, the approach is used for purposes of comparison. Defined only in institutional terms, a comparison would tell us very little. The role of the Supreme Soviet in the foreign policy of the Soviet Union, for example, can hardly be compared with the role of its counterpart in Britain, the House of Commons, still less with the Congress in the USA. The approach enables us to compare pressures and demands on decision-makers wherever they arise; psychological factors that will affect key decision-makers whoever they may be, and so on. Thus we may compare the access of the military to key decision-makers in the United States, the Soviet Union, and Nigeria and discover common pressures that they characteristically exert, or we may compare the problems of command and control in the bureaucratized foreign policy systems of western Europe. Such comparisions are not merely desirable but, as is clear from the approach of all these chapters, actually necessary in the pursuit of any understanding of the phenomenon of foreign policy.[9]

PROBLEMS OF THE FOREIGN POLICY SYSTEM

The uses we can make of the system approach, however, also point to consequent drawbacks. The fruitfulness of behavioural systems demands analyses of great complexity and there is no obvious way of deciding on the limits of relevance. Even a brief consideration of *Figure* 2.2 indicates the formidable depth of analysis that is required to describe the perceptual dimensions of the system. In its entirety, the foreign policy system makes impossible demands on the student of the subject if it is organized as a behavioural system of action. Indeed at its extreme, behaviouralism, as Roy Macridis has said, 'provides the worst possible answer — study everything'.[10]

A second problem heightens the first, It is not possible to disaggregate the system to study only certain parts of it without doing violence to the central notion that it represents a *process*. It cannot be studied piecemeal without reducing it to no more than a static framework. It is possible, of course, to concentrate on particular aspects of the 'inputs' or 'outputs' as McGowan and Shapiro have done in their research, covering topics such as the role of personalities, leadership recruitment, economic and social factors as far as they are observed to affect foreign policy; as component parts, in other words, of the whole system.[11] Such studies, however, can only be judged on their own merits, not as partial explanations of the policy process. They may fit into the system framework and may contribute to other explanations, but in themselves they are not *about* the definition and explanation of the system. The uncomfortable fact is that when we attempt to utilize the foreign policy system for explanation we have to take the thing as a whole and try to make sense of it as such.

A third problem involves the 'operationalization' of the system. This results in what has been called the 'problem of dynamism'.[12] The dilemma is that the system cannot be applied to the real world at the level of detail required, say, by *Figure 2.2* as a whole; yet when parts of it are operationalized as a first step to something more ambitious, it loses its necessary dynamism. Roy Jones has pointed to this problem: 'The dynamics of this basic system are those of the merry-go-round, full of movement but essentially unchanging and stationary.'[13] A more telling illustration is provided by Brecher's work. Having outlined a sophisticated model of the foreign policy system in Israel, a second work tried to operationalize the system by studying seven particular policy areas over the twenty year period.[14] Impressive as these works undoubtedly are, they still do not fit easily together and they cannot satisfactorily account for the dynamic and continuous process of Israeli foreign policy-making. At best, they can only say how the system worked on a number of particular occasions.

Finally the foreign policy system approach may be criticized for its methodological limitations, on the grounds that it does not in fact offer explanations, except at a level of abstraction that makes it unhelpful; it can be no more than an arrangement of components. In other words, it is certainly not a theory for it can only suggest what *might* be relevant. It cannot specify relationships directly or offer causal explanations.

Many writers have expanded upon such problems and maintained that they prevent the approach being translated into 'operational research' on foreign policy.[15] Such criticisms, however, do not render the foreign policy system useless. Rather, they indicate how the approach should be properly used. The system is not trying to explain everything that happens in foreign policy. That would be impossible, so the idea of a general foreign policy system is not very helpful. We must therefore make *assumptions* about how the system might operate at a certain level, or in relation to a particular problem. No single explanation is adequate to deal with the complexity of foreign policy, but a series of assumptions can yield a number of possible explanations which give some insight into *regularities of behaviour* in a certain context. In this way the use of the systems approach is an aid to understanding. The task of defining and clarifying the assumptions that can be made about the operation of the system has been tackled with a good deal of success by students of foreign policy over the last twenty years. Our ability to articulate different sets of assumptions about the way a foreign policy system might work has been one of the most tangible advances in the field of foreign policy analysis.

ASSUMPTIONS OF FOREIGN POLICY SYSTEMS

In keeping with the principles of the approach, any assumptions we make must be applicable to the whole foreign policy system. To assume a 'rational' policy, for example, is not simply to say that key decision-makers acted rationally, but that the whole system operated in such a way as to *allow* them to do so. The concept of a system, therefore, is a device to follow through an assumption about how the foreign policy process might be seen to work. All the concepts, models and paradigms that have been outlined to account for the workings of the system are derived from certain assumptions. In general they fall into two broad categories. If we understand the implications of these, then most of the work on foreign policy systems falls conceptually into place.

Formal Political Assumptions

What may be called formal political assumptions emphasize the importance of 'strategic' decisions. 'Strategic' is not used here necessarily in a military sense, but refers merely to key policy decisions which set foreign policy on a particular course of action. Strategic decisions are the most obvious form of decision that can be observed. The system reacts to such decisions and they involve a deliberate choice between alternatives, a matter of allocating values, on the part of the key political leaders. The issues that Brecher examines, for instance, include the problems for Israel of Jerusalem, the Jordan Waters issue of the 1950s, and the Six Day War, among others. He distinguishes between 'strategic', 'tactical' and 'implementing' decisions in all cases and is in no doubt that strategic decisions exist, that they represent important political choices and are known to be so by the authoritative individuals who make them.[16] The system is assumed to operate so as to structure and define inputs in terms of alternatives that embody various political values that the society reflects. A choice is authoritatively made and perhaps upheld in subsequent decisions, and implementing agencies are then involved in a series of less politicized decisions which give effect to the strategic choice. These assumptions do not deny that a great deal of foreign policy is a messy flow of inchoate actions at all political levels, but it stresses the degree to which this continuous process is moulded and determined by certain periodic and decisive political choices. The importance of the role of individual leaders (though not necessarily constitutionally determined ones) is clear in such assumptions. The notion of a *decision* is at the centre of this view of the foreign policy system.

A clear example of such assumptions being born out by practice might be provided by President Nixon's decisions over Vietnam in 1972. In order to increase pressure on the Hanoi negotiators to be more cooperative in talks to end the Vietnam war, the political leaders of the United States took a decisive gamble in May by stepping up the bombing of North Vietnam and then mining Haiphong harbour to prevent Soviet and Chinese supplies reaching North Vietnam. In taking such steps the decision-makers were calculating that this would not prove too provocative to

Hanoi's allies and in particular that it would not jeopardize the signing of the first Strategic Arms Limitation Treaties planned with the Soviet Union. These calculations proved to be correct.[17] Important choices were being made here between genuine alternatives, and likely reactions were being considered as part of a more overall picture of objectives. The decisions were 'made' by the system as a whole in providing information and interpretation upon which the calculations were based, but the decisions were actually 'taken' by those who were formally responsible for them. While there continued to be a flow of American actions in relation to Vietnam, there can be no doubt that these strategic decisions determined much of what was subsequently done.

In the same way, the British government took a series of strategic decisions in relation to the Falklands crisis of 1982. British policy prior to the invasion on 2 April was not at all strategic; it was marked by a distinct lack of clear and authoritative choices at an appropriate political level. Once the crisis broke, however, the Thatcher government reacted in a highly strategic way. Key decisions were taken; to despatch a task force to show that Britain was prepared to fight, to augment it massively as it became clear that it would have to, to sink the *General Belgrano*, and to launch the land invasion of the islands. Throughout more than two months there was a constant flow of alarms and confusions. But at critical points in all of this key decisions were taken, by the appropriate leaders, who considered the alternatives as best they could and opted for a clear course of action.[18]

From these general assumptions several perspectives have been drawn. The familiar 'strategic perspective' of foreign policy, with all its associated ideas, is the most obvious. Thus the state is seen as a unitary actor in the world, leaders must express some consensual national values and objectives and pursue them by engaging in the game of 'statecraft'.[19] This traditional perspective would simply not make sense unless leaders were assumed to make genuine decisions.

A more specific application of the assumptions is the

democratic perspective of foreign policy-making. In general this is concerned with the extent to which foreign policy processes are consistent with public control and accountability. Hence it must assume that certain leaders who are held responsible for foreign policy are, in fact, making decisions. The essence of democratic foreign policy is that alternative courses of action are perceived, and one course is held to be more consistent with social values than others. So democratic leaders are charged with taking acceptable strategic decisions in response to inputs that are filtered through channels which are subject to representative action.[20]

A good example of this perspective is Frankel's examination of British foreign policy where he defines the political system as having to respond to changed circumstances after 1945 and he traces the functioning of the system in response to these challenges through the workings of a British political élite, the political parties and public attitudes.[21] Similar assumptions as to which relationships are important are made by Waltz in his study of democratic foreign policy in Britain and the United States.[22] While he does not articulate an explicit foreign policy system, he is nevertheless concerned with patterns of influence and communication between electors and executive agencies and in particular with the functioning of political parties in relation to government. Neither writer is saying that Britain and the United States are models of democratic foreign policy but both writers are obviously applying the yardstick of formal political assumptions as standards by which democratic systems can be measured. Such assumptions provide the clues as to where to look for the expression of values, channels of influence and so on, for this is one way in which the system can be seen to operate.

A wider, and undoubtedly the most popular, perspective to be drawn from these general assumptions, however, is that of rational decision-making. This is a more behavioural and less explicitly normative perspective than the democratic one, but it derives from precisely the same assumptions. This offers clues as to its implicit normative elements. The decisions of the Nixon Administration in 1972, or the Thatcher Government in 1982, could be explained according to this perspective. The key to it is not just that leaders make decisions, but that decisions are the result of a *process of analysis*. In ideal terms the system acts to outline and analyse the possible alternative courses of action and the decision-maker will then choose the optimal course.[23] The system is thus perceived as acting according to an intellectual process, and though its information may be wrong, or its interpretation faulty, an analysis takes place and action is therefore *purposeful*.

The danger of allowing this general perspective to be labelled a 'rational actor model' lies in the implications of the concept of rationalism, for 'rational' is often confused with 'right'. If a foreign policy goes wrong we often say that the decision-makers acted irrationally. But whether right or wrong, if the decision was an act of analysis it can hardly be irrational. We could only judge a decision to be irrational where an actor defined certain choices, adjudged one of them to be the most appropriate, and then for reasons of cussedness or perversity, did something different. Though world politics may appear to be populated by cussed and perverse leaders, we can hardly say that these are the prime motives behind faulty decision-making.

Rationality is an ambiguous notion in this context and this perspective is better understood merely as purposeful, analytical decision-making.[24] The importance of the problem of rationality is that it highlights the inadequacies of this sort of perspective. If a genuine decision cannot be actually irrational, *action* obviously can be, as in the case of automatic reaction, anger or pique. This leads us to question whether decisions, as formal acts of analysis, should be given as central a place as they are here. It is logical to consider what the non-decisional mainsprings of foreign policy action might be, since formal political assumptions, while continuing to be important, nevertheless leave significant gaps. In response to this, a number of perspectives have been drawn from what we may term 'administrative assumptions' about policy-making.

Administrative Assumptions

Various insights and ideas have been borrowed from management science and the study of organizations to cope with the problems of sheer complexity in modern foreign policy.[25] The problem of accounting for the dynamic elements in foreign policy is rendered even greater as the system responds to more elements more quickly and interdependently. Since leadership can be seen to be increasingly difficult in modern politics so formal political assumptions, which derive so much from a faith in explicit leadership, can only express a part of the phenomenon. The focus, therefore, has shifted away from the foreign policy system as a mechanism for leaders to articulate political values and choices, towards a concentration on the system as a management structure. Writers making these sort of assumptions have typically been more concerned with the output, rather than the input side of the system. There has been a growing interest in the elusive aspects of implementing decisions rather than in the more institutionally-based study of taking them. Writers note the often tenuous connections between what governments say they intend to happen and what does actually appear to happen; between what is expressed as policy and what impact it has when translated into action.[26]

Stated simply, administrative assumptions about how foreign policy processes operate are based on the fact that single important decisions are actually very hard to find. The vast array of outputs from a foreign policy machine — posturing statements, individual actions by diplomats, provision of money and goods — cannot be convincingly traced back to such clear decisions. Indeed, leaders' decisions can only account for a small proportion, and perhaps not even the most important, of the system's output. Moreover, even when decisions *are* seen to be made by leaders they may not involve a *real* or *conscious* choice. They may not constitute a real choice because genuine alternatives may not be presented at the point of decision: they may not constitute a conscious choice because individuals cannot always know at the time the significance of their actions. If a real choice cannot be consciously made, then we are not studying an act of analysis or a decision at all.

Foreign policy actions, however, do not happen entirely at random, so it is necessary to adopt assumptions which place the mainsprings of action elsewhere. Examples are not hard to find. A number of well-known illustrations, both trivial and important, are offered by Allison in relation to certain actions in the Cuban missile crisis. One of the clearest indications that the Soviet Union was installing medium range ballistic missiles (MRBMs) in Cuba was that surface to air missiles (SAMs) to protect the MRBM sites were installed and arranged ostentatiously in exactly the same trapezium-shaped patterns as within the Soviet Union. This offered direct evidence to the Americans that MRBMs were likely to be introduced, since the deployment of SAMs in this way could hardly mean anything else. A formal political explanation would assume that the discovery of the sites was what Soviet decision-makers intended, or at least that they understood the implications of discovery and had integrated them into their strategy. 'What', it was asked at the time, 'are the Soviets up to in not being more careful?' Allison suggests, however, that we know the transportation of the SAMs was the responsibility of Soviet military intelligence and the KGB, but that the construction of the SAM sites once they were on the island was a highly technical job performed by the Air Defence Command. And the simple fact may be that while military intelligence and the KGB always operated secretly, the ADC did not and always did things this way.[27] So the crucial aspect of secrecy in this part of the Soviet action was probably not the result of a formal decision at all.

The Falklands crisis offers a good example of this too. Though the British government acted strategically and successfully during the crisis, it is interesting to wonder why the Argentinian Junta ever assumed it could get away with an unprovoked attack on the islands. As was obvious after 2 April 1982, the British government never had any intention of relinquishing sovereignty or control. But for the previous two years it had not conveyed that determination to the Argentinian government. Instead it had conveyed the contrary impression. The Ministry of Defence, in order to save money, was in the process of withdrawing the support ship which patrolled the Falklands; the Home Office had introduced a new Nationality Act which, as an unintended by-product, had excluded a number of Falklanders from British citizenship; the Department of Education and Science was running down its meteorological surveys on South Georgia as an economy measure; while the Foreign Office was taking an ambiguous negotiating stance over the Falklands at the United Nations, which may have seemed like the prelude to a major concession. If the Argentinians assumed that all of this was deliberate British government policy, then they had every reason to believe that it signalled a diminution in the British commitment to the islands. But all these actions were not the product of a considered, official policy. In truth there was no real government policy as such, because it was not discussed at Cabinet level. In the absence of political direction each ministry made its own decisions for its own reasons and 'policy' was the result of a series of incremental, unconnected actions by a variety of organizations.[28]

To take a less dramatic example, the British government takes a series of decisions every year on the allocation of its foreign aid budget which dispensed, in 1986, £1420 million across more than 100 countries.[29] The distribution of money within the budget, however, is not the result of a process of overall analysis. Britain is not alone in operating a foreign aid programme that has evolved in an entirely piecemeal way and been structured not around the poor of the world or even the most politically 'useful', but around the former colonies as they gained independence. Foreign aid is regarded as one of the instruments of foreign policy, but the British aid programme is a result of an accumulation of historical circumstances and is very difficult to manipulate in a strategic way. It may be no worse for that, but we should be aware that aid 'outputs' owe more to the ghostly web of past practice and administration than to current authoritative choices.

Another manifestation of the system operating according to administrative assumptions is also worthy of note, though specific examples cannot be given. This is the notion of 'non-decisions'.[30] This does not refer to a decision to do nothing, since this, after all, is still a choice, but it describes a failure to confront a choice, or even to recognize that one exists. For inputs, as we have said, only become problems requiring choices when the system handles them as such. Routine procedures may handle inputs in such a way that this does not happen. Routine produces outputs, so non-decisions do not constitute inactivity, but the continuous flow of activity can serve to channel, dilute, or suppress problems to the point where they cease to exist for the decision-makers.

To take again the example of foreign aid, money may be given to another state, not because of the virtues of a particular project but because it has always received an annual grant and nothing has arisen to question the arrangement. In retrospect it may become clear that a considerable problem is posed by this aid policy (if, say, the aid is used to release other indigenous resources which are spent on dubious arms purchases or a nuclear weapons programme), but the routine nature of the action prevents other relevant information from being collected and considered, and hence effectively prevents the problem from arising in a given period. By the time this is fed back into the system as a problem it may already be too late to alter it.

On the basis of these sorts of assumptions, what perspectives have been adopted to translate them into an explanation of the system's working processes? One of the most influential is the incrementalist perspective associated with the works of Braybrooke and Lindblom.[31] This emphasizes that organizations have to fragment inputs and issues into different problems to be handled by specialists at different levels (as in the Cuba example, transporting and assembling the missiles required different levels of specialism). Officials exercise their rightful discretion and make a series of small decisions according to their responsibilities, but the cumulative effect of this may produce a momentum in favour of one course of action which is irresistible by the time it is considered by a formal political leader. Incremental processes often culminate in a formal political decision but this may only invest authority on a choice that has already been made by lower level actors who were unaware of the cumulative significance of their individual actions.

Clearly related to this is the perspective of cybernetic decision processes. Cybernetics refers to a pre-programmed system of action where a way of dealing with a specified input is predetermined. The most obvious example of this would be the action which flows from a computer programme. This has been related to human activity in the way in which people have to deal with routine.[32] The British Foreign Office handles a daily two-way traffic of 3000 telegrams alone, all of which require some sort of action. Officials cannot consider each one analytically, certainly not in any depth. They have to act according to habit and instructions. Thus an official in any bureaucracy will often respond with a mental 'reflex action'; only a very restricted range of options are considered when a minor choice has to be made (for example, who should see this telegram, how quickly does it require a reply?); the choice between them will be made on the basis of a 'trigger' such as a key word or phrase which leads one to assume what the information is about and what should be done with it; and the criterion of acceptable choice will not be the optimum expected outcome but the *first* satisfactory one that fulfils the basic responsibilities of the official. While this perspective has evolved from routine decision-making, it has also been applied to cumulative decision processes at a higher political level. For the essence of cybernetics is the principle of 'satisficing' — not searching for the optimal course but for the first acceptable one that gets the issue off one's desk, and this can apply to leaders as well as officials.[33]

The most influential perspectives based on these assumptions are probably the organizational and bureaucratic politics 'models' of the foreign policy process. Both of these have existed for some time but have been characterized by Allison as two alternative formulations to rational (analytical) actor assumptions.[34] An organizational perspective builds on the premises of incrementalism by assuming that organizations are dominated by their 'standard operating procedures' which will only occasionally be waived or breached. Above all, it stresses that foreign policy actions will not necessarily be determined without analysis or reason, but that the analysis may not be a unified or overall one consistent with more formal assumptions. Organizations may well act perfectly logically and clearly within their own standard operating procedures and responsibilities, but there is no guarantee that their outputs will be consistent or compatible within the foreign policy process as a whole. The criteria for analysing choices will be internal to the particular organization, as opposed to being internal to the foreign policy process. So, in searching for the political values that guide decisions, we need to look at the subtler mixture of roles and motives that may affect quite low-level decision-makers – officials who on formal assumptions would be regarded as merely 'implementers'.

Bureaucratic politics, examined in Chapter 5, extends this perspective to account for actions not by way of the different workings of organizations within the bureaucracy, but by the assumption that their necessary incompatibilities will be heightened and developed as a struggle between them. Officials, in this view, are not at all unaware of the significance of their actions and, seeing national interests through the eyes of their role in their departments, will do all they can to have that view prevail over others. A foreign policy decision, therefore, may be the result not of any single view of the national interest, it may not have much to do with the intrinsic merits of the problem – even in times of crisis – but may merely represent the only acceptable compromise between competing bureaucratic interests.

The bureaucratic politics perspective has commanded a great deal of support – and criticism – over the last twenty years and many studies have borrowed from it to account for certain aspects of the working of a particular foreign policy process, even of decision-making in international organizations.[35] We need only note here, however, that while bureaucratic politics has tended to dwarf the looser concept of organizational politics, it is nevertheless the latter which has better stood the test of time and academic scrutiny. Bureaucratic politics is probably best regarded as a particular variant, applicable in precise circumstances, to the more generally ubiquitous perspective of organizational politics.

USING DIFFERENT PERSPECTIVES

These constitute the main assumptions that have been applied to foreign policy systems. The perspectives derived from these assumptions see the policy process as operating in characteristic and differing ways. How do these perspectives help us? First, they make explicit the fact that what we are examining is a system of *action* not necessarily of *decision*. Many foreign policy actions have very tenuous links with direct political decisions, and to explain them we have to do more than study the stances of key political leaders. Or, expressed another way, we may say that decisions, if they do determine foreign policy, as Brecher claims, nevertheless come in all shapes and sizes: some will be direct and vital; some will merely rationalize existing practice; some will be clear, some deliberately ambiguous; some will be 'holding' decisions merely to buy time; some will be impossible to implement, others intended to be seen to fail; some will be decisions to let others decide, and so on. In this light, to say that foreign policy processes are about 'making decisions' does not say very much. We still need to understand the flow of actions and procedures of which those decisions form a part — and often only an indirect part. There are many other determinants to action besides the key decision-makers.

Second, we should be aware that the outputs of foreign policy systems are by nature rather amorphous and will be more difficult to characterize than purely domestic outputs. Of course, domestic and foreign policies are becoming increasingly indistinguishable in the modern world, but the point still holds, for when domestic policy is projected on to the international screen it loses much of its clarity. It becomes more long-term and will tend to merge into wider, less tangible packages of issues that are more characteristic of foreign policy. Foreign policy outputs are difficult to evaluate and categorize because they have less calculable (though no less real) results on their environment.

Third, we can see that these perspectives overlap. Each is saying something about the whole system — from inputs to outputs and feedback. But the system which each of them describes — an analytical decision system, a system of organizational action, a system of cybernetic action, or whatever — is too neat to match the complexity of real-world foreign policy. We should recognize, therefore, that there are elements of all types of action in virtually every foreign policy issue; the system acts in all these ways simultaneously. At some points the analytical aspects of the process may assume more importance, at others, a bureaucratic battle may emerge which dominates the problem and becomes itself the issue — to be resolved in turn by an act of leadership at some future stage.

Foreign policy systems are engaged in a constant search for an acceptable method of making political, analytical decisions. In a sense, rational or analytical decision-making stands as an ideal to which decision systems aspire. The conditions in which foreign policy operates, however, make this goal impossible. For the student of foreign policy the trick is to be able to analyse which factors are more important determinants at a given time; to be able to spot when political leadership *is* making its presence felt, or when it is only ratifying what has been arrived at incrementally, and so on. In a study of United States policy towards the Arab-Israeli dispute, for example, William Quandt argues that from 1967–76 presidential leadership was assertive on four distinct occasions. While these were important occasions, for the remainder of the time organizational factors and bureaucratic battles were probably the chief determinants of United States policy.[36]

This point is most dramatically illustrated by the concept of 'crisis'. A crisis only exists if the system acts as if it does. For a crisis has been said to involve the elements of time pressures, heightened threat perceptions and genuine surprise, and all of these are internal to a foreign policy system.[37] Crisis are exactly those occasions when we should expect a foreign policy system to act analytically: key political leaders become continuously involved, more information is generated, there is less time for discussion and a necessity to act quickly. On the face of it we might expect that this situation would favour more analytical decision-making. This point has been strongly made by Spanier and Uslaner who argue that this is 'particularly reasonable' to explain crisis decisions.[38] This, however, is a misleading characterization to the extent that it overstates the power which leaders – even United States presidents – can, in practice, exercise.

Research on crisis decisions indicates that they embody many other elements of action and cannot be accounted for by the analytical perspective alone. Spanier and Uslaner maintain that national interests are at stake in a crisis, thus political leadership must emerge strongly and consultations will be restricted. This is undoubtedly true, but it does not follow from this that action will be more analytical. Leaders depend crucially on information in a crisis, and the lack of the right sort of information can render them incapable of making choices. Equally, the overload of information, in which the most salient facts are lost in what is known as the 'background noise' of a crisis, can also induce a paralysis of leadership. Both of these are matters for the organizational processes of a foreign policy machine: the speed with which it can gather the relevant information and the skill with which it can process it in a crisis.[39]

Conversely, a lack or an overload of information in a crisis has also been observed to heighten the anxiety of leaders and may induce in them a predilection to act for the sake of it. In acting in this way they are likely to draw from past experience and stereotypes, rather than the current situation, which they cannot formulate. This can be seen to be a form of cybernetic reaction, where choices are made by key leaders but according to certain 'triggers', derived from previous cases. There were large elements of this in the American reaction to the *Mayaguez* incident in 1975 where a Cambodian gunboat seized an American freighter off the coast. The President and Secretary of State took the lead in sending marines to rescue the crew of the ship at exactly the point at which they were being released peacefully. Whatever information the decision-makers were operating on, it is clear that they did not try to obtain all that was relevant and easily available, and were reacting, in the wake of the final collapse of South Vietnam, to the trigger that a US ship had been pirated by Communist forces.

In short, no one type of issue, not even a crisis, can be satisfactorily characterized by one perspective of policy-making. Leaders will be heavily involved, but they do not always promote analytical decision-making. Their genuine decisions must be set in a broader context which raises other possibilities. To do less is to underestimate the difficulties which political leaders face.

CONCLUSION

The foreign policy system is a framework that allows us to organize our study of the subject. In itself it can tell us nothing directly since when it is written down it can only be a list of variables. Having compiled such a list, however, we then have to decide how they *might* operate and this forces us to be explicit about what assumptions we are making and what perspectives can be derived from them. If the search for understanding must, ultimately, be intuitive, then the proper use of the system approach is an aid both to clarity and insight, for it allows us to differentiate and explore a number of possible lines of explanation, which collectively can enable us better to understand the nature of foreign policy.

NOTES

[1] Tolstoy, L., *War and Peace*, vol. 2, Harmondsworth, Penguin Books, 1957, p. 142.
[2] ibid. p. 876.
[3] For the development of systems theory in the study of politics and foreign policy see Easton, D., *A Framework for Political Analysis*, Englewood Cliffs, NJ, Prentice-Hall, 1965: Easton, D., *Varieties of Political Theory*, Englewood Cliffs, N J, Prentice-Hall, 1966, ch. 7: Almond, G. A. and Powell, G. B., *Comparative Politics: A Development Approach*, 2nd edn, Boston, Little, Brown, 1978: Deutsch, K. W., *Nerves of Government*, New York, Free Press, 1963. On the application of systems to foreign policy see Modelski, G., *A Theory of Foreign Policy*, London, Pall Mall, 1962: Rosenau, J. N., *The Scientific Study of Foreign Policy*, London, Francis Pinter, 1980: Jones, R. E., *Analysing Foreign Policy*, London, Routledge & Kegan Paul, 1970: Wallace, W., *Foreign Policy and the Political Process*, London, Macmillan, 1972.
[4] For some of the earlier expressions of the methodological force of the approach see Knorr, K., and Rosenau, J. N., eds, *Contending Approaches to International Politics*, Princeton, NJ, Princeton University Press, 1969: Haas, M., and Kariel, H. S., eds, *Approaches to the Study of Political Science*,San Francisco, Chandler, 1970. For later appraisals of the status of the methodology see Parkinson, F., *The Philosophy of International Relations*, London, Sage, 1977: Little, R., 'The Systems Approach' in Smith, S, ed., *International Relations*, London, Basil Blackwell, 1985.
[5] The best general criticism is still that of Bull, H., 'International Theory: The Case for a Classical Approach', *World Politics*, 18 (3) 1966, pp. 361–77.
[6] Brecher, M., *The Foreign Policy System of Israel*, London, Oxford University Press, 1972; and *Decisions in Israel's Foreign Policy*, London, Oxford University Press, 1974. See his later works also in Brecher, M., ed., *Studies in Crisis Behaviour*, New Brunswick, NJ, Transaction Books, 1979.
[7] See, for example Holsti, K. J., *International Politics: A Framework for Analysis*, Englewood Cliffs, NJ, Prentice-Hall, 1978.
[8] See, Moorhouse, G., *The Diplomats*, London, Cape, 1977, pp. 123–4.
[9] On the general aspirations of comparative study see Holt, R.

T., and Turner, J. E., eds, *The Methodology of Comparative Research*, New York, Free Press, 1970; McGowan, P. and Shapiro, H., *The Comparative Study of Foreign Policy: A Survey of Scientific Findings*, London, Sage, 1973.

[10] Macridis, R. C., 'Comparative Politics and the Study of Government: The Search for Focus', *Comparative Politics*, 1 (1), 1968, p. 81.

[11] McGowan and Schapiro, op. cit. See also East, M., Salmore, S., and Hermann, C., *Why Nations Act*, London, Sage, 1978.

[12] Dawisha, A. I., 'Foreign Policy Models and the Problem of Dynamism', *British Journal of International Studies*, 2 (2), 1976, pp. 128–37.

[13] Jones, op. cit. p. 86.

[14] Brecher, M., *Decisions in Israel's Foreign Policy, op. cit.*

[15] The original expressions of this can be found in Singer, J. D., 'The Level of Analysis Problem in International Relations', in Rosenau, J. N., ed., *International Politics and Foreign Policy*, New York, Free Press, 1969. More recent discussions can be found in Mansbach, R., and Vasquez, J., *In Search of Theory*, New York, Columbia University Press, 1981: Hermann, C., Kegley, C., and Rosenau J. N., eds., *New Directions in the Study of Foreign Policy*, London, George Allen & Unwin, 1987.

[16] Brecher, *Decisions in Israel's Foreign Policy*, op. cit. 'Introduction'.

[17] See, Kissinger, H., *The White House Years*, London, Weidenfeld and Nicolson, 1979, pp. 1174–94: Nixon, R. M., *The Memoirs of Richard Nixon*, London, Sidgwick & Jackson, 1978, pp. 733–6.

[18] The best account of the interaction between the confusions and the choices is provided by the *Sunday Times* Insight Team, *The Falklands War*, London, Sphere Books, 1982.

[19] Lovell, J. P., *Foreign Policy in Perspective*, New York, Holt, Rinehart and Winston, 1970.

[20] See, Shlaim, A. *et. al.*, *British Foreign Secretaries since 1945*, London, David and Charles, 1977, ch. 1; Lindblom, C. E., *The Policy-Making Process*, Englewood Cliffs, NJ, Prentice-Hall, 1968, ch. 12; Barber, J. *Who Makes British Foreign Policy?* Milton Keynes, Open University Press, 1976.

[21] Frankel, J., *British Foreign Policy 1945–1973*, London, Oxford University Press, 1975, ch. 2.

[22] Waltz, K. N., *Foreign Policy and Democratic Politics: The American and British Experience*, London, Longmans, 1968.

[23] A good summary of the process of analytical decision-making is offered by Coplin, W. D., *Introduction to International Politics: A Theoretical Overview*, 2nd edn, Chicago, Rand McNally, 1974, ch. 2. Also, Lerche, C. O. and Said, A. A., *Concepts of International Politics in Global Perspective*, 3rd edn, Englewood Cliffs, NJ, Prentice-Hall, 1979.
[24] On rationality see Frankel, J., *The Making of Foreign Policy*, London, Oxford University Press, 1963, ch. 12; Auma-Osolo, A., 'Rationality and Foreign Policy Process', *The Yearbook of World Affairs 1977*, London, Stevens, 1977; Steinbruner, J. D., *The Cybernetic Theory of Decision*, Princeton, NJ, Princeton University Press, 1975.
[25] A summary of these antecedents is provided by Dunsire, A., *Implementation in a Bureaucracy*, vol. 1, London, Martin Robertson, 1978, ch. 2.
[26] See, for example, Allison, G. T., *Essence of Decision*, Boston, Little, Brown, 1971; Allison, G. T. and Szanton, P., *Remaking Foreign Policy; The Organizational Connection*, New York, Basic Books, 1977; Halperin, M., *Bureaucratic Politics and Foreign Policy*, Washington, DC, The Brookings Institution, 1974.
[27] Allison, *Essence of Decision*, op. cit., pp. 110–13.
[28] See *Falklands Islands Review*, Cmnd. 8787 'The Franks Report', London, HMSO, 1983, pp. 76–7.
[29] Central Office of Information, *Britain, 1988*, London, HMSO, 1988, p. 126.
[30] Bachrach, P. and Baratz, M., 'Decisions and Non-Decisions: An Analytical Framework', *American Political Science Review*, 57 (3), 1963; Lukes, S., *Power: A Radical View*, London, Macmillan, 1974.
[31] See Braybrooke, D. and Lindblom, C. E., *A Strategy of Decision*, New York, Free Press, 1970.
[32] Steinbruner, J. D. *The Cybernetic Theory of Decision*, op. cit.; see also Inbar, M., *Routine Decision-Making*, Beverley Hills, Calif., Sage, 1978.
[33] On 'satisficing' see Simon, H. A., *Administrative Behaviour*, New York, Macmillan, 1959.
[34] Allison, op. cit.
[35] Cox, R. W. and Jacobson, H. K., *The Anatomy of Influence: Decision-Making in International Organization*, New Haven, Yale University Press, 1974, ch. 11. See also typical examples of bureaucratic studies in Halperin, M., *Bureaucratic Politics and*

Foreign Policy, op. cit.; Quandt, W. B., *Decade of Decisions: American Policy Towards the Arab–Israeli Conflict 1967–1976*, London, University of California Press, 1977; Neustadt, R., *Alliance Politics*, New York, Columbia University Press, 1970.

[36] Quandt, op. cit.

[37] See Hermann, C. F., *Crisis in Foreign Policy*, New York, Bobbs-Merrill, 1969, pp. 29–30.

[38] Spanier, J. and Uslaner, E. M., *How American Foreign Policy is Made*, 2nd edn, New York, Praeger, 1978, ch. 4, esp. pp. 104–39.

[39] See Hermann, C. F., ed., *International Crisis: Insights from Behavioural Research*, New York, Free Press, 1972; Janis, I. L., *Victims of Groupthink*, Boston, Houghton Mifflin, 1972; Bell, C., *Conventions of Crisis*, London, Oxford University Press, 1971. For the best brief summaries see Oppenheim A. N., 'Dynamics of Decision-Making' in Open University workbook D203, Block 7, Part 4; or his chapter in Groom, A. J. R. and Mitchell, C. R., eds, *International Relations Theory: A Bibliography*, London, Pinter, 1978.

3. The Context of Foreign Policy Systems: The Contemporary International Environment

DAVID ALLEN

Chapter 2 has drawn our attention to the notion of a foreign policy system functioning within two environments, internal and external. The land mass of the world is now almost exclusively divided up into states, each of which is identified by the possession of, among other things, a government claiming legal sovereignty over its territorially defined space. If we take the state as our central focus of attention, within which the foreign policy-making process is located, then the internal environment is limited by the territorial boundaries of the state and all that falls outside those boundaries, and hence outside the formal authority of the state, makes up the external environment. Although, as noted in Chapter 1, it is becoming increasingly difficult to maintain a rigid distinction between political behaviour within any one state and that outside it, as well as between governmental policies directed towards these two environments, it nevertheless remains the case that the boundaries themselves continue to exist and, for the purposes of our analysis, have meaning.[1]

The external environment of any one state in the system fundamentally encompasses all the other states in the system, both individually and in a variety of combinations. We have already noted, however, that within and between all the states in the system there also exist entities known as 'non-state actors'. These include international organizations (both governmental like the United Nations and non-governmental like Amnesty International), multinational companies like IBM or Unilever and transnational political and religious movements such as the Communist Party or the Roman Catholic Church.

All such non-state actors, like state actors, can create inputs from the external environment into any foreign policy system or systems that we happen to be considering. Inputs from the external environment may not necessarily be transmitted directly to the formal decision-making centre. For instance, a foreign government may choose to exert pressure on a target government either through an intermediary in the domestic environment or by seeking to influence domestic public opinion. Although the legal distinction that marks the division between the two environments remains clear, it is now generally accepted that even the most powerful and relatively autonomous of states are vulnerable to 'penetration' of one sort or another from outside. In other words, the neatness and absoluteness of the distinction between the two environments is lost because governments can no longer exclusively control the flow of information and ideas across the boundaries that mark out their areas of authority.

A foreign policy system approach makes certain assumptions about the relationships that exist between states and the contemporary international environment. It makes it difficult to accept the notion, prevalent among some international relations theorists, that states are the total prisoners of their environment: states are seen as exercising, with varying degrees of success, some sort of choice as to their external behaviour. To accept the notion of choice in foreign policy and then to go on to look at the ways in which choices are perceived and decisions taken and implemented, is to reject the determinism of the 'billiard ball' or 'macro' approach to the study of relations between states.[2] From that perspective, where the emphasis on the structural properties of the international environment leads to propositions about the nature of state behaviour 'demanded' by the environment, there is little need for foreign policy analysis.[3] All states are regarded as being fundamentally captured by the imperatives of the international system and thus their behaviour, albeit at the most general of levels, supposedly becomes predictable. If there is one thing that students and practitioners of foreign policy have learnt over the years it is the difficulty of predicting states' behaviour, particularly if one wishes to move from broad generalizations towards specific instances; that is why we continue to search for ways of comprehending the complexity and idiosyncracy of foreign policy behaviour.

This, of course, is not to deny the influence of the structure, or rather structures, of the international environment on the activities of states. Singer has ably demonstrated the problems inherent in concentrating exclusively on the individualistic nature of particular states and of assuming that their behaviour can be explained entirely in terms of domestic processes.[4] As in most areas of the social sciences, the task of describing, understanding and explaining behaviour demands a balance of what can be termed the 'micro' and 'macro' views of the problem. Thus we need to take account of much of what has been written about the structure of the international system, for it is of relevance to our understanding of the external environment provided that we recognize the dangers of over-simplification and over-generalization as well as the essential distinction between influence and determination. In fairness, many of those writers who choose to concentrate on the structural properties of the international system recognize the limitations of this approach. Morton Kaplan, for example, has argued that his famous models of international systems are not meant to be predictive models of foreign policy processes. He argues that:

> to expect that the loose bi-polar model would explain behaviour in the African sub-system when it is designed to explain the overarching system of international politics would be equivalent to expecting a model of monopolistic competition to explain the economics of the garment trade on the East Coast of the United States.[5]

Before examining the characteristic features of the contemporary international environment, one further point needs to be made about the relationship between the environment and the foreign policy system. Many of the features of a state's internal environment can only be regarded as significant when considered in relation to the external environment. The power of a state, for example, can only be evaluated in relative rather than absolute terms, and this cannot be achieved by the popular textbook method of producing absolute ranking lists of various categories of resources and capabilities that are then aggregrated to give a crude measure of a state's power.[6] It is argued here that both analyst and foreign policy-maker are required to evaluate a state's internal capabilities in relation to the international environment or at least to relevant parts of that environment. Thus, the military capability available to a policy-maker does not represent a measurable asset in its own right but acquires significance only in terms of the forces available to other relevant states or, indeed, in respect of prevalent attitudes in the international environment towards the use of such a capability. Similarly, the effectiveness of a particular form of bureaucratic organization for the formulation of foreign policy decisions can only be evaluated properly in respect of the performance of that organization in interaction with other actors in the international environment. Events and processes in the international environment will only acquire significance and relevance to a particular state to the extent that they are viewed in terms of the internal or domestic characteristics of that state.

Thus, although we must now go on to discuss the

international environment in highly generalized terms, it is important to remember that there is no such thing as one 'objective' external environment that can be linked in the abstract to a foreign policy system. Quite apart from the problems of differing perceptions on the part of decision-makers in an increasingly heterogeneous collection of states, each state in the international system has its own distinct international environment by virtue of its unique geographical position and combination of material and human assets. There is, therefore, a certain danger in promoting the notion of the external environment and in particular of attempting to evaluate the significance for a general model of foreign policy of certain trends, changes and developments in that environment once one accepts that these things will have different meanings for different states. This problem is made more difficult by the fact that much of the writing on the nature of the contemporary system emanates from sources which are fundamentally in tune with the interests of the advanced industrialized states, and in particular those of the western capitalist world. Thus a development such as decolonization, which was regarded in the West as representing a fundamental change in the external environment, was not so regarded by those states who saw the underlying links between the ex-imperial states and their former colonies to be unbroken despite certain constitutional changes. It is also the case that most western writing on the international system shows a bias towards a notion of order that is dependent on the rough preservation of the international status quo, whereas for many of the states in the less developed world the main focus of interest in the international environment is not how an unjust order is to be preserved but rather how it might be changed in the interest of greater equity.

Despite the reservations mentioned above and accepting the biases prevalent in the literature, it should still be possible to attempt a characterization of the contemporary international system that is of some relevance to any state that has to operate within it. To this end we shall need to consider its scope and structural characteristics, the nature of its various participant units, or actors, and the various ways that they interact with each other as well as the extent to which those interactions are restrained by either formal or *ad hoc* rules.

THE SCOPE AND STRUCTURE OF THE INTERNATIONAL ENVIRONMENT

There is a sense in which the external environment of any one state now encompasses the whole world, if only because scientists who have developed the notion of a 'nuclear winter' argue that there is literally no place on earth that would be safe from the horrific aftermath of a nuclear war. Less dramatically, it is now possible to travel from one point on the globe to another within a relatively short period of time. Intercontinental missiles can do it in under an hour, the airlines in less than a day. It is quite possible for any one state to be in virtually instantaneous communication with any other state although, of course, the ease and frequency of contact can still vary enormously between the 160 plus states that make up the contemporary system. Symbolic of the fact that the international system now includes the entire landmass of the globe is the existence of the General Assembly of the United Nations in which, with a few exceptions, all states can gather and debate issues with one another. Thus the present system is a truly global one in which all states are at least aware of each other's existence even if, at any given time, they may not all choose formally to recognize one another. There are no longer any 'hiding places' on the planet and so it is not possible for any state seriously to contemplate a foreign policy of isolation based on a rejection of all contact with its external environment, or on an assumption of immunity from the influence of developments in that environment. It can be argued that this state of affairs is likely to continue and that the speed of communication and the level of shared knowledge within the system is likely to increase rather than diminish. The only possible frustration of this continued 'globalization' might occur in the aftermath of a devastating nuclear war: then it might well be the case that the scattered survivors of such a holocaust would begin to rebuild their civilizations in complete isolation from one another.

The fact that the entire habitable landmass is now occupied with states that have some form of contact with one another does not of course mean that the setting for the conduct of international politics is now complete. Just as in the past international actors vied with one another for control of the seas for purposes of navigation, so now they are beginning to contest the ownership of the resources that either live in or are to be found below the seas. So too, some of the states in the system are beginning to explore outer space and to visit other planets. Both these developments involve the extension of the external environment because all states, whether directly involved or not in these activities, will be indirectly affected by the way that these 'new territories' are developed and controlled. Although in the past the hope has been expressed that in these new areas of the international environment the benefits and attendant responsibilities might be shared by all under the guidance of some sort of international authority, it seems increasingly likely that they will be the object of exactly the same sort of interstate competition and division that characterizes our management of the landmass.

To observe that the international system has now expanded to include the whole world and that it may shortly be extended into space is not, of course, to suggest that we are witnessing a growing global integration or an improvement in the quality of relations between states. A greater awareness of the nature and scope of the external environment has not led to any greater appreciation of a harmony of interests. In fact the opposite would seem to have occurred. Actors and systems of actors that had previously existed in peaceful ignorance of one another have found that contact and mutual awareness has led to conflict and suspicions, as we shall see when we examine the common forms of interaction that characterize the contemporary system. Thus the expansion of the system has presented policy-makers within any one state with a new set of external challenges and potential misunderstandings. The larger and more complex the system becomes and the greater the number of issues and events that are the substance of international politics, the harder becomes the job of those who have to try and make sense of it all in order to make foreign policy. Indeed the external environment has become so complex that there can be few certainties and few ways of imposing control even for the most powerful of states. Even the superpowers have demonstrated in recent years that their decision-makers have problems in dealing effectively with more than a few selected aspects of the international environment at any one time. Although there is a vast amount of information, affected by varying degrees of distortion, flowing around the system at any given time, all participants are handicapped by an inability to handle it in such a way that interests can be identified and choices made. To know about the extent and complexity of the contemporary system is no guide to behaviour, and so foreign policy-makers in all states find themselves forced to simplify and select in order to try and maintain the impression of understanding and control. For most states in the system this means that their participation can only be partial and limited either geographically or to certain types of issue that are of particular concern.

There are, therefore, considerable disparities between states in terms of the extent of their active participation in the system. Although, as we have seen, all states have the potential for a minimal involvement with any other state, in practice the most intense activity tends to take place at the regional rather than the global level.[7] Even the two superpowers have to reconcile their competitive interest in global developments with their particular regional responsibilities in western and eastern Europe and with their particular security concerns in, say, Central America and Afghanistan respectively. For most other states, whether concerned about their security or anxious to exploit collaborative opportunities, the regional rather than the global arena will probably prove to be the most relevant. A characteristic of the external environment of most states will thus be the existence of regional substructures within which interactions will be more intense than at the global level.

All international systems, including the present one, are also characterized by disparities in the extent of power and influence of their constituent parts. The major powers have always exerted great influence over the conduct of relations between all other states in the system and their particular configurations are said to form the basic structural framework within which all states are forced to operate. The period since 1945 is notable for the domination of the system by the two superpowers, the United States and the Soviet Union, both of whom possess nuclear and other military capabilities that no other state in the system can aspire to match. Analysts continue to argue as to whether the competition that has existed between these two powers since 1945 is a product of their adherence to conflicting ideologies or the inevitable consequence of their participation in a system that is characterized by a bipolar structure. Whatever the cause, the conflict between the two superpowers has dominated the environment of all other states in the system. At its height, states found themselves effectively forced to choose between alignment with one of the two superpowers or membership of a non-aligned movement that arose in reaction to their overbearing dominance. However, this period has now passed and in many ways the grip of the two superpowers appears to be slackening even though the alliance structures that they created continue, albeit in the face of growing internal division.

During the 1970s, however, international relations theorists went too far in assuming that a fundamental shift in the structure of world power had taken place.[8] During the heady days of detente, and to a certain extent in response to the overblown claims of the Nixon Administration, many came to believe that economic power had replaced military power as the most important source of influence in the system. Much was written about the impact of interdependence on sovereignty and on the new role of transnational, non-governmental actors.[9] With the Strategic Arms Limitation Treaty (SALT I) in the bag, the Vietnam war concluded and the European Security Conference about to take place, it was as if the end of the cold war had been announced. It seemed to many that the major schism in the system was no longer between East and West but between North and South and that the major structural challenge was to devise, not a stable nuclear relationship, but a 'new international economic order'. As it turned out, events towards the end of the decade, culminating in the Soviet invasion of Afghanistan and the election of a US President determined to pursue East–West competition with renewed vigour, showed that no such revolution had taken place in the external environment and that the structure of global military power remained important.

It is clear, nevertheless, that in the contemporary international environment there is no longer one basic structure that dominates the international system, for power and influence are no longer solely related to military strength. While both superpowers continue to deter each other with their formidable nuclear capabilities, they have both experienced difficulties bringing either nuclear or conventional military predominance to bear on lesser adversaries such as the North Vietnamese or the Afghan rebels. Similarly, at the global level, the United States has been forced to concede economic influence to states such as Japan, West Germany, and to a lesser extent Iran and Saudi Arabia who are militarily less powerful; while politically, both superpowers have to cope with the growing influence of western Europe, China and regional groupings such as the Arab League and the Contadora states.

The structure of global power has become disaggregated to such an extent that there are almost as many hierarchical structures as there are issues.[10] The United States and the Soviet Union remain predominant at the nuclear level, the global structure continues to be bipolar and is stabilized by the willingness of both superpowers to negotiate with one another. There is no room within this structure for new power centres to play a significant role nor is there likely to be in the foreseeable future. On the other hand, the international economic system has been in a state of relative anarchy following the breakdown of the structure of order based on the Bretton Woods agreements.[11] Here three major power centres can be identified: the United States, Japan and West Germany/western Europe represent roughly equal centres whose attempts to collaborate in order to provide stability and order in the system have so far failed. It is in the international economic system that inter-state relationships are most complicated by the activities of non-state actors such as banks, companies, share and foreign exchange dealers. Indeed one of the major power centres, western Europe, might be said to be handicapped by the fact that it is not a state.

Foreign policy-makers, therefore, are faced with a bewildering array of hierarchies at both the global and regional level. Useful allies on some issues can become unhelpful opponents on others, while states whose dominance in one area might lead them to expect successful outcomes in another, instead find themselves frustrated. It thus becomes difficult for leaders to predict the likely course or outcome of various conflicts of interest within their external environment, and the multiplicity of hierarchical structures inhibits the attempts of both academics and policy-makers to predict behaviour from simple models of the environment. Power may remain the criterion for constructing patterns of influence, but the definition of power, never an easy task in the more straightforward world limited mainly to military and diplomatic interactions, becomes an even more complex task in the contemporary system.

THE NATURE OF THE ACTORS AND THEIR INTERACTIONS

It has already been established that foreign policy is an area of governmental activity and that, therefore, our central focus of attention is the state; for it is only in association with the state that we find governments. We have also argued that for any state, a major part of its external environment consists of the governmental activities of other states in the system. This, however, is not the same thing as suggesting that the only inputs into the foreign policy system emanate from other governments or that governments have an exclusive monopoly or control of all boundary-crossing activities. In addition to the 160 or more states that exist today, we can identify numerous other actors operating above and below the level of the state whose behaviour is of relevance to foreign policy analysis. As states remain our central focus these other actors become significant, not only in their own right, but to the extent that their behaviour affects or influences governments.

Many writers have argued otherwise, however, and claimed that the central role of the state itself is challenged by the existence of non-state actors in the contemporary environment. In particular, it has been argued that the smallest and weakest of states in the system, which are usually distinguished by having a population of less than a million — the 'micro states' — are not viable, economically, politically or militarily, in the face of challenges, both from other larger states and from more powerful non-state actors such as multinational companies or transnational movements. It is possible to argue that all states have now become vulnerable to penetration both by modern weaponry and by transnational forces, such that their original *raison d'être* — the exercise of sovereignty over a piece of territory — is no longer valid.[12] We shall examine both states and non-state actors in order to support the contention here that, while the latter obviously exist and are of significance in the external environment, they can still be contained within a state-centric framework.

First of all there is ample evidence that the state as a unit of organization continues to thrive in the contemporary system. Not only has there been a considerable expansion in the number of states in the twentieth century as the European empires have broken up, but the scope of governmental activity and hence intergovernmental activity has expanded. Furthermore, and perhaps as a reaction to interdependence, the force of nationalism that originally formed the basis of the state system does not seem to have abated despite the existence of transnational political, religious and social forces. The free flow of communication that characterizes the contemporary system has led observers to regard, for instance, the Roman Catholic Church or Muslim fundamentalism, the international Communist movement or the international student movement as potential threats to the territorially based state. That such forces impinge on the foreign policy considerations of governments cannot be denied. At the beginning of the 1980s many states in the so-called 'arc of crisis', including the Soviet Union, found their interests threatened or enhanced by the sweep of the Islamic revolution; just as in the 1960s student rebellion had swept across a number of advanced societies and forced them to adjust their internal and external policies.

States do not remain static in the face of these challenges, however, and just as some governments use their sovereign power to resist these forces by censorship, restriction of individual rights and other counter-activities, so others have successfully 'nationalized' these forces. Thus, following the Sino–Soviet split and the evolution of European Communist parties, it is perhaps debatable whether one can seriously identify a world Communist movement. Just as multinational companies have shown themselves anxious to conform to local practices and to recognize national sensitivities, so the Roman Catholic Church has shown itself willing to accept conditions laid down by individual states in order to continue the practice of its faith. It is not unreasonable to expect that after the first flush of revolutionary fervour, much the same process of 'national secularization' will weaken the transnational impact of Muslim fundamentalism.

There are, of course, occasions when nationalism, encouraged by other interested states, threatens the existing political structure, but usually the prime objective of groups struggling for 'national liberation' is the establishment of new or altered states. Thus the existence of such forces and the availability of support for them does present a challenge to certain states but not to the state system itself. The Palestinian Liberation Organization (PLO) is certainly a non-state actor whose influence affects the interests of those states who are either committed to Israel or are concerned about the supply of oil from sympathetic Arab states, or who are generally in favour of the creation of peace and stability in the Middle East. The PLO and similar organizations are a significant part of these states' external environment.

Much the same argument can be advanced when considering other non-state actors. Multinational companies have proliferated in recent times to such an extent that writers in the late 1960s argued that by the year 2000, some 300 such companies would 'rule the world'.[13] While it is certainly the case that many of the world's largest companies now command assets that are considerably greater than the gross national products of many of the smaller states, and while their activities are of great relevance to those governments whose policies they may affect, they nevertheless remain subject to the laws of the country in which they operate. In many cases governments have shown themselves capable of managing the activities of companies either by threatening or carrying out nationalizations or by cooperating with other governments to prevent companies exploiting differences in such things as tax rates or investment incentives. Rather than challenging the state system itself, multinational companies have on occasions proved to be the willing accomplices of their parent states, serving effectively as part of the foreign policy apparatus. In this way the Chilean government of President Allende became only too painfully aware of the fact that not just the official representatives of the US government but the management of the US multinational ITT were anxious to see it fail.[14]

In seeking to maintain their authority, governments have created a number of international organizations at both the global and regional level, many of which have themselves come to be regarded as significant actors in their own right in the international environment.[15] In the 1980s there are some 200 governmental and 2000 non-governmental organizations registered with the United Nations (UNO). Although many of these organizations are limited in their freedom to act by the veto power of their members, they nevertheless represent both a challenge to and a new forum for national foreign policy-makers, even if they do not represent a fundamental challenge to the existence of states in the system. These organizations are indicative of the growing interdependence that characterizes the contemporary international environment and although many of them were set up by states anxious to preserve rather than to cede their sovereignty, they can all, regardless of exactly how they take their decisions, be seen as behaviour 'modifiers'. From time to time certain organizations are regarded as having been 'captured' by one state or a grouping of states. For example, the UN has been seen in the past as an extension of United States interests and these days as sympathetic towards the less developed majority of its members. This rarely proves to be a permanent feature of organizations, however, so that all can be seen as playing some sort of autonomous role in the system. At the global level the UN family of predominantly welfare organizations, and at the regional level organizations like the European Community or the Arab League, make up an important part of the international environment which states cannot afford either to disregard or to completely reject when considering their foreign policy objectives and the best means of attaining them.

Although states remain the primary focus of attention for other states in the contemporary international environment, they are by no means a homogeneous set of entities. Apart from the great disparities of size, wealth and hence influence that exist among states today, it is also the case that they vary considerably in terms of ideology and form of political organization. Although it is crudely possible to distinguish between superpowers, medium powers, small powers and micro powers, it is also necessary for any one state to consider the other states in the system in terms of whether their political systems are 'open' or 'closed', whether their economies are developed, developing or underdeveloped or whether their leaders owe their position to inheritance, to party allegiance, to democratic election or to all three. If they are to operate effectively in the international system, one-party states are expected to comprehend the significance of elections and coalition formation in multi-party states, female prime ministers are required to negotiate with countries that accord no political status to women, and former guerrilla fighters find themselves requesting aid from leaders who had previously participated in forceful attempts to deny them political power. In these and many other ways the disparate nature of the states that make up the contemporary system presents a formidable challenge to those responsible for the conduct of foreign policy for they are required to identify, protect and advance the interests of their states when confronted by unfamiliar value systems and organizational processes.

We have so far established that while states remain dominant actors within the system and military security issues still continue to be of great importance in relations between states, neither hold a monopoly on foreign policy-makers' attention. In the contemporary international environment we can identify three types of international transaction: intergovernmental, transgovernmental and transnational. *Intergovernmental* interactions consist of direct dealings between governments which, we have argued, have greatly increased as a result both of the expansion in numbers of states and the broadening range of issues that are the subject of direct government-to-government relations. This increase in activity has led both to an increase in the number of accredited diplomats in the system and the participation in foreign affairs of those officials and politicians who in previous periods would have restricted their activities to the internal or domestic arena.

In recent years there has also been a tendency for the multilateralization of direct government contacts to occur. While many issues are still the subject of bilateral dealings, the existence of international organizations and of *ad hoc* international fora has led to the development of new styles of conference diplomacy. Within formal institutional structures such as the European Community, the North Atlantic Treaty Organization (NATO) or the United Nations, informal processes have arisen so that states are faced with the formidable task of comprehending and selecting the best arenas in which to identify and advance their interests. When, for example, the British government was faced with the task of responding to the oil crisis in the 1970s, it chose to pursue what could be seen as contradictory options.[16] Direct bilateral dealings with the individual oil producers led to conflicts with Britain's fellow members of the European Community who were attempting to share the misery and thus counter Arab attempts at selective punishment. At the same time, Britain was forced to respond collectively as a member of the European Community to requests from the Arab oil producers for a Euro-Arab Dialogue. The Europeans also had to arrive at a common position and the result of this was to distance the EEC members from the United States, producing further conflict within the NATO Alliance and leading the Americans to believe that their chances of exploiting western solidarity in dealings with the Middle East had been undermined. Thus, the availability of multiple, overlapping fora makes intergovernmental dealings additionally complex.

In the contemporary system governments are not necessarily coherent policy-making units. Other chapters in this book draw attention to the fact that different elements within governments find themselves in competition with one another over the selection of goals and the means of pursuing them in the international environment. This tendency produces a second category of interactions which we can describe as *transgovernmental*. Here government departments and agencies deal directly with their opposite numbers in other governments sometimes in defiance of their national policy positions. It has often been noted for example, that the agricultural ministers of the European Community, in their regular meetings with one another, display a mutual transgovernmental solidarity in their determination to spend money on farm support, regardless of the wishes of their colleagues at home. Similarly, it has sometimes been noted in arms control negotiations between the United States and the Soviet Union, that while the Soviet and US leaders may share the common objectives of reaching agreement, they may be frustrated by the fact that their respective military representatives share a common interest in not reaching such an agreement. The growing web of transgovernmental contacts, which are most intense between the advanced industrial societies, and particularly those in western Europe, are a feature of the external environment that can both be exploited and regarded as an inhibition by governments seeking to maintain coherence in their stances towards the outside world. In receiving inputs from the external environment, governments are faced with the task of determining whether they represent actual policy stances held by other states or merely attempts by one sector of a foreign government to exert influence within its own domestic environment. All this makes the task of interpreting messages from the external environment that much more difficult.

Finally, in considering the activities of the various non-state actors discussed above, we can describe their boundary-crossing activities as indicative of *transnational* interaction. These actors will seek to influence events, both by dealing directly with one another and by seeking to negotiate with government decision-makers. Their real influence is harder for governments to determine because of their ability to exploit indirect international channels of communication and in particular because of their ability to penetrate directly the internal or domestic environment of a state. In some cases they are able to disguise what is effectively an input from the external environment as an internal demand.

Having established the various ways in which international interactions are channelled, we must now say something about their substance. The external environment is typified by relations of both conflict and collaboration. Although interdependence and the dangers of escalation to nuclear war would appear to put a premium on states cooperating with one another, violence remains a constant feature of interstate relations. Although the major powers appear to have reached a position of stalemate in that their possession of weapons of mass destruction inhibits the use of force in their dealings with one another, they are still inclined to arm other states with conventional weapons and to attempt to exploit their own conventional military strength in their dealings with non-nuclear states. It is only really among the states of western Europe that force, or the threat of force, has lost its utility and even these states are not inhibited from using force outside their own continent or in threatening to use force in order to deter the supposed threat posed by the Soviet Union and the states of eastern Europe. All other states in the system show no real reluctance to use force to resolve disputes or to advance interests, and wars of a covert and overt nature have broken out and can be expected to break out in every region but western Europe. Though even here Greece and Turkey have come close to war in recent years.[17]

At the same time, states have exhibited a growing willingness to explore the possibilities of peaceful cooperation. Although their potential competition with one another now extends to include a much wider range of issues than in any previous system, the growth of formal and *ad hoc* international organizations and the expansion of collaborative ventures stand as evidence that there is more to international life than mere survival in a world of totally competitive and inevitably hostile neighbours.[18] What might be challenged, however, is the view that the development of cooperative as well as conflictual behaviour indicates a move towards some sort of integrated global system. John Burton has convincingly demonstrated what he regards as the 'fallacy of the continuum', whereby he sees no natural organizational or behavioural development which would suggest that states in the system can be expected to form regional entities that would eventually lead to a world government.[19] It is also true that many of the examples of cooperation in the external environment are themselves built on wider conflictual relationships. Thus the European Community was founded by states with a mutual fear of the military power of the Soviet Union and the economic power of the United States. The Community now pursues policies such as the Common Agricultural Policy (CAP) or the completion of the internal market, which seem designed to achieve internal unity by a process of relative isolation from the rest of the international system. Similarly, both NATO and the Organization of Petroleum Exporting Countries (OPEC) are good examples of states which choose to work together but which owe their solidarity to their mutual suspicion of and hostility to other groups in the international system.

Moreover, states in the contemporary system have found ways other than using force to pursue conflictual rather than collaborative relationships.[20] The post-war period has seen not just a proliferation of wars 'by proxy' in which states like the USA and the Soviet Union have fought each other indirectly via client states, but also a growth in the willingness of states to interfere in each other's domestic processes even to the point of sponsoring terrorism and subversion. Technological developments have enabled states to develop the art of spying on each other and the use of propaganda has become widespread, not just as a specialist 'tool' of foreign policy but as part of a new type of 'declaratory' diplomacy which has served further to complicate and distort the process of sending messages in the contemporary international environment. Finally, the use of economic threats and rewards has proliferated with the application of economic sanctions of one sort or another. These have become an almost irresistible and acceptable 'gut reaction' when states disagree with one another, even though there are few examples of economic sanctions achieving anything other than symbolic objectives.

Thus, although conflict and collaboration are dual features of the external environment, one type of behaviour does not appear to advance at the expense of the other. Indeed states seem to find relationships that exhibit both tendencies quite acceptable even if they take some explaining to their respective domestic constituencies. The United States and the Soviet Union have continued to discuss means of controlling their nuclear arms even during the course of the Vietnam and the Afghanistan conflicts. The West Europeans and the Americans, fellow allies when it comes to warding off the Soviet threat, regularly threaten each other with all manner of economic deprivations in retaliation for supposed slights. The contemporary environment cannot be said then to be characterized by one prevalent form of behaviour, and simplistic generalizations about the way a state should conduct itself in order to protect and advance its interests are of little help to contemporary foreign policy decision-makers.

RESTRAINTS AND RULES IN THE CONTEMPORARY INTERNATIONAL ENVIRONMENT

When we turn to consider the existence of a body of rules and restraints in the international environment, we find a further reason for maintaining a state-centric view of international relations. To the extent that elements of consensus exist within the external environment, it is fair to suggest that they exist among states rather than any other groupings. While certain groups of human beings may agree about the definition of human rights and while there may be a consensus within capitalist states on the correct way of indulging in commerce and profit-taking, it is not possible to find any generally accepted ways of behaving that would enable us to talk of a global society of human beings. It is possible, however, following the arguments of Hedley Bull, to talk in terms of a society of states.[21] Despite the great differences among states that we have identified, a certain degree of consensus does appear to bind them all together and condition their dealings with one another such that it is not possible to view the international system as completely anarchic. The rules of diplomatic conduct, for example, that were developed by the European powers in an earlier period have come to be broadly accepted by the entire community of states, even though they are more frequently abused and distorted these days than in the past. Diplomatic protocol provides a common language for easing communication between states with differing value systems, cultural traditions and means of expression, and all states in the contemporary environment have to a greater or lesser extent recognized that they have an interest in maintaining contact, often via third parties, even with states with whom they are at war. War itself has come to be regulated by international laws on the treatment of prisoners, on respect for neutrality, and by agreed limitations on the use of chemical and biological and, for some states, nuclear weapons. There appear to be tacit agreements among the major powers in the system about the acceptable extent of their respective spheres of influence and, despite the fact that there is no world authority to police it, a substantial body of international law exists and is in the main upheld by the majority of states. The legal sovereignty of states, both internally and externally, is a fundamental value that is admittedly abused but never fundamentally challenged and even in times of conflict most states demonstrate an anxiety to justify their actions to their fellow inhabitants of the planet.

Apart from the agreed formal and tacit rules and restraints on state behaviour, the absence of either a world government or a working system of collective security ensures that the major powers at the global, regional and local levels have particular roles to play in the management and preservation of the system of independent states.[22] In other words security for most states is guaranteed by their conscious participation, either alone or in informal or formal alliance with other states, in an attempt to preserve the balance of power and thus prevent any one state coming to dominate a particular locality, region or indeed the global system itself. Although preserving the physical integrity of territory remains a fundamental value for all states many, particularly those in the developed world, have come to define their security more broadly and have thus had to attempt to preserve the status quo in a whole series of complex power relationships.

Consensus in the contemporary environment is challenged by a conflict between notions of order and of change.[23] With regard to the rules and restraints in the system, there is a constant struggle between those who demand change and those who see their interests best preserved by the maintenance of the status quo. These two notions are often quite incompatible such that change of any sort is seen by some as subversive of order, while the institutions of international society are seen by others as designed to favour certain types of states to the permanent exclusion of others. As we have seen, the international environment, in the absence of world authority or a global system of collective security, shows conflicting tendencies of both anarchy and society. Opinions differ as to whether the present system shows any particular leaning towards one extreme or the other, but the task of making policy within such an external environment is made considerably more difficult by the uncertainties that exist about the operating rules of conduct within the system. It is perhaps for this reason, above all others, that academics continue to make a distinction between political life within and between states and thus to separate for the purposes of analysis the internal or domestic, and the external or international environments within which the foreign policy of a state is conducted.

NOTES

1 Wallace, W., *Foreign Policy and the Political Process*, London, Macmillan, 1971, Introduction and ch. 5.
2 Wolfers, A., 'The Actors in International Politics' in *Discord and Collaboration*, Baltimore, Johns Hopkins University Press, 1962.
3 Buzan, B., *People, States and Fear: The National Security Problem in International Relations*, Brighton, Harvester, 1983, pp. 101–5.
4 Singer, J. D., 'The Level of Analysis Problem in International Relations' in Knorr, K. and Verba, S., eds, *The International System: Theoretical Essays*, Princeton, NJ, Princeton University Press, 1961.

[5] Hopkins, R. and Mansbach, R., *Structure and Process in International Politics*, New York, Harper and Row, 1973, p. 138.
[6] Spanier, J., *Games Nations Play: Analyzing International Politics*, 4th edn, New York, Holt, Rinehart and Winston, 1981, pp. 129–67.
[7] Coplin, W., *Introduction to International Politics: A Theoretical Overview*, Chicago, Markham, 1971, ch. 12.
[8] See in particular Keohane, R. and Nye, J., *Power and Interdependence*, Cambridge, Mass.,Harvard University Press, 1977.
[9] Huntington, S., 'Transnational Organizations in World Politics', *World Politics*, 24 (3), 1973, pp. 333–68; Keohane, R. and Nye, J., *Transnational Relations and World Politics*, Cambridge, Mass., Harvard Univeristy Press, 1971.
[10] Pirages, D., *Global Ecopolitics: The New Context for International Relations*, North Scituate, Duxbury, 1978.
[11] Gilpin, R., *The Political Economy of Internutional Relations*, Princeton, NJ, Princeton University Press, 1987.
[12] Herz, J., *International Politics in the Atomic Age*, New York, Columbia University Press, 1959. Herz's thesis was later modified in Herz, J., 'The Territorial State Revisited: Reflections on the Future of the Nation State' in Rosenau, J., ed., *International Politics and Foreign Policy*, New York, Free Press, 1969, pp. 76–89.
[13] Spero, J., *The Politics of International Economic Relations*, London, Allen and Unwin, 1977, pp. 88–115.
[14] Berridge, G., *International Politics. States, Power and Conflict Since 1945*, Brighton, Wheatsheaf, 1987, pp. 23–35.
[15] Taylor, P. and Groom, J., *International Organisation: A Conceptual Approach*, London, Pinter, 1978.
[16] Lieber, R., *Oil and the Middle East War: Europe and the Energy Crisis*, Harvard, Harvard Centre for International Affairs, 1976.
[17] Knorr, K., 'On the International Uses of Military Force in the Contemporary World', *Orbis*, 21 (1), 1977, 5–27.
[18] See Morgenthau, H., *Politics Among Nations*, 5th edn, New York, Knopf, 1972.
[19] Burton, J., *International Relations: A General Theory*, Cambridge, Cambridge University Press, 1965, pp. 55–67.
[20] Berridge, G., op. cit. pp. 55–127.
[21] Bull, H., *The Anarchical Society*, London, Macmillan, 1977.
[22] ibid. pp. 101–27.
[23] ibid. pp. 77–100.

4. The Context of Foreign Policy Systems: Environment and Structure

CHRISTOPHER FARRANDS

It is not difficult to illustrate the importance of the context within which foreign policy is made. No American president can ignore for very long the pressure and demands of domestic values, whether they are expressed directly to him or through Congress, through the media or through lobbies. British foreign policy-makers have had to adapt to declining economic influence over more than forty years. Problems created by the balance of payments and the strength or weakness of sterling have been enduring constraints on foreign policy. The foreign policies of many African countries have been shaped by drought as well as by their internal politics. Alternatively, when Eygpt emerged as an independent state after the 1952 revolution its government was committed to a programme of internal development which, coupled with nationalism, created very high expectations among the Egyptian people. Given also Egypt's position within the regional balance of power, though, it is possible to conclude that the government had very few real 'choices' to make, formal independence notwithstanding. Or again, Mexico and Austria can no more ignore their superpower neighbours than Japan can ignore the fact that it has become a major force in the world economy.

While these random examples illustrate the importance of the environment within which the foreign policy system operates, they also demonstrate the problem which any student of foreign policy faces when looking at the environment. How can these diverse structures and processes be understood? Systems theory suggests that we can conceive of relations between the environment and the foreign policy system as a series of interlocking and interacting systems. To develop the idea of interacting systems, however, it is necessary to specify their boundaries, to examine their character and to explain the process of interaction between different environmental systems. That is the task of this chapter and it is undertaken in three stages. First it examines in some detail how 'traditional' foreign policy analysts set up the problem of relations between the policy process and the environment. Second, it considers more briefly a specific problem at the heart of an understanding of the role of the environment, namely the issue of determinism. Finally the chapter sets up a general framework for understanding the relationship between foreign policy and the environment and suggests how it might be applied.

THE TRADITIONAL POLICY–ENVIRONMENT RELATIONSHIP

Traditional foreign policy analysts, who can be taken here to include many decision-making theorists working in this field, draw two important distinctions when discussing the relationship between foreign policy and the environment.[1] First they distinguish between the *domestic* and the *international* environment. The domestic environment of policy is different from the international environment because the nature of politics within the state is very different from politics in the international arena. In international politics there is no single source of law, although law exists and is important. The international system is an anarchical one where power and authority are widely spread and where the key institutions, such as the balance of power, the practice of diplomacy and war, and the principles of state recognition and sovereignty, provide a foundation on which expectations about behaviour can be based.

In the domestic environment, authority and channels of policy implementation are clearer. There is normally a single established framework of power and authority. Politics and administration can take place effectively within this framework, whether the principle of government is democratic, monarchical or based on an ideology which sustains a one-party state. The boundary between the external and the internal economy is also seen as relatively sharply marked, though traditional analysts tend to see their subject as primarily concerned with states and their pursuit of power rather narrowly defined.

A second basic distinction is drawn between the *psychological* and the *operational* environments of policy. The psychological environment comprises the policy environment as policy-makers understand it. It includes their perceptions, images, assumptions and expectations about the world. Indeed it is only through their understanding of their circumstances that decision-makers can act. So, for example, Chinese foreign policy is, in part, a consequence of a particular view of China's history of relations with outside powers and the view which Chinese leaders over three millenia have held of their role within that perceived environment.[2] More specifically, China's intervention in the Korean war was a result of its leaders' particular interpretation of the threat which US military successes in September–November 1950 posed for them.[3]

The psychological environment is not unreal. It is not fantasy, except perhaps in very few cases. Hitler later in his career; Napoleon in the last 'hundred days'. The psychological environment is an expression of a reasoned attempt to come to terms with a complex and changing world 'outside', which will include necessary simplifications and possibly mistaken analogies. But if policy-makers do not simplify and draw analogies, they will understand nothing. Constant self-criticism, institutional procedures to check on interpretation, and continuing interaction with the 'outside world' through policy implementation, may all help to narrow the gap between intepretation and reality. But the gap remains as an important source of policy failures. Thus, Wohlstetter has traced the causes of the failure of both United States and Japanese policy assessment in the six months before the Japanese attack on Pearl Harbor in 1941.[4] Both sides had a great deal of information about the other, but because of the assumptions which each brought to their intelligence assessment, they misread the intentions of the other. They did not 'blunder into war'; they carefully miscalculated their way into a war while very accurately understanding each other's core interests. More recent case studies by Janis on the United States failure in the Bay of Pigs attack on Cuba in April 1961; by Shlaim on the Israeli Cabinet's surprise at the Egyptian attack in October 1973; and by Lebow on the British inability to predict the Argentinian attack on the Falkland Islands in April 1982, all suggest that the notion of the psychological environment remains a key focus for students of foreign policy.[5]

The operational environment, on the other hand, embraces the 'reality' outside the foreign policy system, as opposed to interpretations of it. Traditional foreign policy analysts have held the view that, although it is impossible for policy-makers to grasp that reality themselves, an objective account of it is possible. They understand the operational environment to include a wide range of inter-related factors, including social structure and culture, physical and economic environments and, of course, the structure of the international system.

The *social structure and culture* of a country has a strong influence on foreign policy though that influence may not be felt directly in day to day decision-making. Social structure, however, provides a framework of values which policy-makers are likely to share. Nationalism, Islam, fundamentalist Christianity, welfare state social democracy or a distinct racial identity, all constitute frameworks of ideas which make demands on policy-makers. Each ideology has implications for foreign policy even if those implications are not explicit. Values can generate demands for action, or constrain the kinds of strategies that policy-makers can pursue.[6] Thus a social structure which places special emphasis on military values is likely to encourage those values in foreign policy, as Argentina's policy in the 1970s illustrates. Alternatively, Sweden's emphasis on aid policy illustrates the priority that social democratic states tend to give to development issues. Values also provide criteria for the judgment of success or failure in foreign policy. When values change, foreign policy is also likely to change over time. West Germany, for example, altered its policy towards eastern Europe between 1963 and 1969 as a result of the emergence of a new generation of voters and political activists who did not remember 1945 and who wanted a more active normalization of relations in Europe in place of the static cold war policies pursued by the Adenauer government in the 1950s.

More generally, patterns in foreign policy have been attributed to patterns in domestic structure. One version of this view is to argue that 'open' or democratic societies tend to have one kind of foreign policy, while 'closed' or authoritarian societies have a different kind of foreign policy. This argument is characteristic of much comparative politics theory in the 1960s. It appears to have some attractions because it looks like a clear distinction. Indeed Smith and Williams use the distinction to argue that the 'viability' of foreign policy can be explained in terms of open or closed models of society.[7] Thus closed societies can adapt more quickly to change in the international system because they can, in the short term at least, ignore domestic political constraints which might operate in a democracy. Stalin found it easy, for example, to sign the 1939 treaty with Hitler's Germany. Though, as Smith and Williams add, open societies may well find it easier in the longer term to adapt because they have the legitimacy to make changes democratically acceptable and can thus maintain a viable relationship between foreign policy and the domestic public.

This kind of argument is too general, however, and can easily be refuted. Domestic change in China during the Cultural Revolution in the mid-1960s indicated an unstable, closed society: but Chinese foreign policy changed relatively smoothly as China moved first into a period of intense domestic upheaval and then into a period of *rapprochement* with the West. By contrast, French foreign policy in the mid-1950s was severely affected by the Algerian war. The resulting domestic turbulence which brought de Gaulle back to power in 1958 hardly fits the model of viable long-term change in an open society. Furthermore it is possible for relatively open societies to have intensely closed foreign policy systems, as the British obsession with official secrecy illustrates, or as the secret war waged by Nixon and Kissinger in Cambodia at the end of the 1960s shows.[8] More recently, in the Iran-Contra scandal, where National Security Council officials used income from arms sales to Iran to support terrorist activities in Central America against the wishes of Congress, the US foreign policy system has again suggested that there is no necessary connection between an open society and an open foreign policy. The relationship between social structure and domestic politics on the one hand, and foreign policy on the other, is real and important, but it has to be analysed in detail and with sophistication. General accounts, such as those which draw on some of the older comparative politics literature, often display a high degree of ethnocentricity or, in the case of theories based on ideas about 'cultural types', even of racism.

Writers are agreed, however, that two general features of social structure and organization are important. Size obviously sets some limits to resources available to foreign policy. Small states may be able to play a significant role in international politics if they are located in a strategic position or if they are sponsored by a major power. The capacity of some small states to act in ways which appear to transcend their resources has attracted a number of studies. David Vital, for example, has looked at the degree of independence which small states can have which may arise from their ability to manipulate their environment or, like Israel and Vietnam, through their ability to impose their will on larger but less purposeful states by virtue of their strength of ideological commitment.[9]

The literature on foreign policy has also conceded a particular importance to the level of development of a state. This may be interpreted in terms of economic development, or more broadly, in terms of social, economic and political development. As with other themes in comparative politics, this may tend to ethnocentric argument, though not necessarily. In an interesting case study on Ugandan foreign policy in the early 1970s, Maurice East has pointed out that size is perhaps less important than the qualitative differences between levels of development and the levels of bureaucratization which this may involve.[10] While some developing states, such as India or Egypt, have large, highly competent bureaucracies, others generally do not. Developing states as a whole lack the infrastructure of advanced, industrial states and many also have problems of disunity, tribal or religious conflicts usually traceable back to their colonial inheritance, which give a distinctive character to their political processes.[11] Among advanced industrial states the same kind of distinction is made by Edward Morse, who has argued that the process of modernization has transformed the foreign policies of countries such as France.[12] Modernization here means a rapid, destabilizing process of social change combined with economic growth and linked to the internationalization of key sectors of the economy, all of which has important political consequences. In Morse's study of France, these developments were reflected in the modernizing foreign policy of that state in the 1960s. Here a particular formula was pursued which combined technical modernization, rapid economic growth led by state investment, a strong concern for national independence and a dynamic attempt to seize and use the leadership of certain international institutions such as the European Community, while attempting to undermine American influence in others, such as NATO. This formula was in some ways unrealistic to the extent that it seriously underestimated France's ability to shape international relations. But it successfully created a domestic consensus behind a broad strategy in foreign and domestic policy while encouraging necessary and very beneficial developments in the economy.

A very different form of modernization was encouraged in the 1960s and 1970s by the Shah of Iran, who sought to transform his country into 'the fifth superpower' by rapid westernization, economic growth, urban and social reform, all backed by a vicious police system. These programmes were very successful in material terms, but they undermined the established values of that society. The main focus of traditional values, the national religious institutions, became the main agents of a profoundly anti-western, anti-materialist revolution in 1979 which swept away a government that had lost almost all of its earlier supporters.[13] The rate of change, the direction of change, and its implications for social stability all have the most important implications for foreign as well as domestic policy, as the French and Iranian examples in the 1960s and 1970s demonstrate.

The *physical environment* of foreign policy includes landscape, physical size and location, climate and the defensibility of borders. These elements were seen as the determinants of foreign policy by the geopolitical theorists of the early twentieth century.[14] These theorists still have influence on students of military strategy, but they are less important in writings on foreign policy. Nevertheless the physical environment of a state does have an influence on foreign policy: it shapes opportunities and threats to which the foreign policy system must respond. For example, the existence of the English Channel, the size of the two superpowers, the significance of maritime 'choke points' at the Straits of Dover, Hormuz and Malacca, and the relative indefensibility of Poland's borders, have all had a significant role in shaping the course of various conflicts this century. After a decade of fighting in Afghanistan, Soviet policy-makers probably have a much clearer idea of the impact of the physical environment on foreign and defence policy than they had beforehand.

The significance attached to the physical environment, however, can change as a result of a change in how it is interpreted, or as a result of changes in technology. When, for example, the United States moved from the Polaris to the Trident nuclear submarine systems, the much greater range of the Trident missiles meant that US submarines could move from the Mediterranean to the Indian Ocean while still being able to strike at targets almost anywhere in the Soviet Union. Or, to take a different type of example, the development of electronic trading and communications systems have made possible a highly integrated global financial and currency system which reduces the time that governments have to respond to monetary movements. They used to have much longer to respond because of the sheer difficulty of global communication. Thus, the physical environment is not an 'absolute given' in foreign policy. It is possible over time to modify its impact. After the First World War, in which Germany was defeated in part as a result of a very tight economic blockade, German scientists were asked to develop synthetic products which could replace imported goods in an international crisis. Their success meant that an equally tight blockade in the Second World War had far less real impact on the German war economy. The physical environment is an important element in foreign policy, shaping a basic environment which policy-makers have to recognize. But how they recognize it and how they adapt national technologies to deal with it are also important to our understanding of it.

The *economic environment* of policy constrains external relations in two ways which have long been recognized. A basic lack of resources may compel a shift in foreign policy. During the fifteen years after the Suez crisis, British forces were progressively reduced and then withdrawn from 'East of Suez' (the Gulf, the Indian Ocean and the Far East) as the goals of policy were painfully adapted to match the available resources.[15] Immediately after the 1973 Middle East war, the Japanese government came under Arab economic pressure because of its closeness to the United States. At that time Japan imported about 70 per cent of its energy including nearly all its oil. Thus Japanese leaders shuffled with some embarrassment away from the United States on Middle East issues, taking up a position more acceptable to conservative Arab states such as Egypt and Saudi Arabia. This included a recognition of the Palestine Liberation Organization within six months of the 1973 war. In the longer term, Japanese firms have found a very valuable market in the Middle East open to them for the first time, but the initial aim was simply to keep the oil flowing.[16]

A second economic issue in foreign policy has always been the need for resources. In the thirty years before 1945 British weakness East of Suez was already apparent. But imperial resources, especially Indian troops and Indian taxpayers, could make up for British economic weakness at home. In the same period, Japanese economic vulnerability in resource terms was compensated by a careful programme of expansion into a 'Greater East Asian Co-Prosperity Sphere' which was designed to ensure a flow of resources from Manchuria and from Indo-China. Most countries are committed to an active role in international trade by the need for resources. The European Community, for example, may or may not become internally united but it will remain highly dependent on certain imported minerals for the foreseeable future, even if it can become less dependent on imported fossil fuels. By contrast, the United States and the Soviet Union should continue to be largely independent in resource terms, a factor which should help them to continue to play a pivotal role in international relations.

The *structure of the international system* is the final main category of environmental factors. This has been dealt with in detail in the previous chapter, but to complete a review of those factors recognized as important by traditional writers, it is necessary to take note of those aspects of the international environment which bear most immediately on the foreign policy system. In particular, alliance commitments form an important part of a pattern of constraints on foreign policy. It is possible to break a promise to an ally; in some circumstances it may be unavoidable. But to undermine previous commitments involves costs not only to relations with the ally concerned but also to the self-interests which the original commitment embodied. When states shift alliances, it is usually as a result of a long-term and, therefore, predictable change in their interests as, for example, when Italy moved from the Central Powers to the Allies in 1915 or when France left the military structure of NATO in 1966. Sudden breaks are by definition more problematic, except when policy-makers' views of their interests have been transformed by, for example, domestic revolution.

Maintaining an alliance framework brings stability and predictability to foreign policy; it also reduces perceived risks. It is therefore worth considerable effort. British efforts to act as a 'bridge' between the United States and western Europe, although often unsuccessful and nearly always resented, have been worthwhile to British policy-makers to the extent that they have helped to stabilize the key institutional framework within which British foreign policy exists. Informal commitments may carry as much significance as formal treaties. The Soviet Union has felt constrained to support Cuba since the early 1960s for several reasons, including a fear of Chinese rivalry and a perceived opportunity to weaken the United States; but a major factor has also been the need to honour its commitments in the eyes of potential friends and enemies alike.

The existence of the international system itself constrains states, even though they retain their sovereignty. As Hedley Bull has argued, there are rules and assumptions which both reflect the interests of states and which constitute a basic structure of order.[17] Even though individual governments may break these informal rules over particular issues, most states most of the time do follow international norms of behaviour. Not only do they find it convenient, but they can only assert their own statehood by behaving in the way that states are expected to behave. One compelling example of this is the way in which the new Bolshevik government in the Soviet Union soon abandoned its stance of 'revolutionary diplomacy' in favour of a more traditional approach. Henkin has stressed the importance of the framework of rules within which states operate.[18] Many other writers would argue that he is over-optimistic about the real effectiveness of restraints on international wrongdoing; but they would accept his argument that, where such rules do restrain governmental choices, they do so not because they *regulate* policy but because they come to form part of the working assumptions of the policy-makers. The structure of international society, then, together with the alliance and commitment framework within which states operate, form significant elements of an international structure which constrains and shapes foreign policy processes.

That completes a review of the major elements of the environment which have been traditionally regarded as important. These remain relevant factors, as the discussion here has illustrated, but there is another dimension of the policy environment which is becoming recognized as equally significant. This can be referred to as the *knowledge structure*. Knowledge provides a resource which some societies may be able to exploit more successfully than others. Access to knowledge and skills among developing countries is limited. Among other things, this leads them to put a particular emphasis on the United Nations in foreign policy management, since on the whole they do not have the resources to maintain worldwide diplomatic representation. By putting their few experienced diplomats into their UN mission, they can conduct effective diplomacy without the expense in money and human skills involved in maintaining a large number of embassies.[19]

Knowledge also means access to commercial sources of information: developing countries are particularly anxious about the penetration of their societies by satellite television and by imported popular culture and advertising. Knowledge also means access to finance or to relatively cheap sources of credit: or, for those with resources committed outside their frontiers, it might mean the capacity to reduce risks. As Susan Strange has argued, knowledge structures are powerful structures, for knowledge is unevenly distributed and the growth of high technology systems for handling knowledge is changing this structure, giving increasing advantages to those with control over the relevant technologies.[20] Thus, in trying to deal with the international issues posed by the spread of AIDS, the growth of terrorism, the possible shortage of strategic minerals or the October 1987 world stock market crash, those who know more, and can manipulate what others know, have more power. 'Those who know more' may sometimes be state authorities, but they are often large information processing corporations, including the news, television and advertising media which are becoming increasingly transnational in scope and impact.

While some aspects of the knowledge structure are new, some clearly are not. Throughout the history of Christendom the churches have claimed a special control over knowledge including what was defined as valid knowledge and what was seen as heresy. The scientific revolution created new structures of knowledge which the emerging modern state was anxious to exploit and control. Nationalist movements have always claimed to legitimize knowledge (especially in the form of interpretations of history) which they use as a source of power and political control. Political ideologies such as liberalism and communism offer a particular structure of knowledge which poses unavoidable challenges to the foreign policy system of any state. They may well cut across state boundaries to undermine state authority; at the very least, they will shape the agenda and values of actors in international politics. Knowledge and ideology structures, it can be argued, are vital frameworks of foreign policy, not merely peripheral additions to it. Moreover the control of these structures in the contemporary world may well be passing out of governmental hands and into those of a range of transnational actors.

THE PROBLEM OF DETERMINISM

The relationship between the environment and foreign

policy as traditionally conceived remains important, but needs to be adapted and developed to take account of changes in that environment. Before turning to suggest a useful way of structuring the environment-policy relationship, however, a fundamental conceptual problem needs to be addressed. The environment can be seen as a general framework which *affects* policy; or as a pattern which *positively shapes* policy; or as a relatively rigid *constraint*. On the other hand some writers have seen the environment as a *determining force* which can in itself explain foreign policy output. Which is correct? This is not simply an empirical question that we can test; it is a question of how we conceive of the environment in its relations with the foreign policy system.

International Relations has a wide range of more or less determinist theories which focus on the international system. They argue, for example, that the international power structure determines the structure and process of international politics; or, alternatively, that the structure of the international economy determines the nature of international politics. Other theories claim that the structure of relations of dominance and dependence between rich and poor countries in a world capitalist system determines the shape of international politics and the outcomes of conflict or bargaining. None of these are theories of foreign policy as such, but all have consequences for the way we see the foreign policy process. For they all maintain that the foreign policy process is externally determined. Northedge, for example, argues that the system of relations between states and, in particular, the balance of power, shapes foreign policy in all states.[21] While there is obviously a political process within states which mediates between the international structure and foreign policy, if we want to explain state behaviour we have to look primarily at the international power structure. Albert Hirschman, in a study which has had a great influence both on 'neo-realist' writers and the international political economy school in the 1980s, argues that the structure of international economic relations shapes the structure of power relations.[22] The argument that a dominance/dependence structure shapes both political and economic relations between states is characteristic of what is called dependency theory.[23]

The basic assumptions of foreign policy analysis, however, include the view that there is an element of choice in decision-making, however limited it may be, and the assumption that internal factors can be at least as influential as external factors on decisions.[24] Thus it can be argued that foreign policy analysis is simply incompatible with determinist theory, and that the analyst has to choose whether to develop a view of international relations grounded on determinist ideas or on ideas which admit an element of choice in human affairs. Structuralist theories which argue that choice is highly constrained by structure, a view which tends towards determinism without being strictly determinist, may nevertheless still be important. It is not difficult to point to cases where states have very tightly circumscribed choices in foreign policy. Even the most committed liberal would have to accept that countries with desperately few resources, such as Nepal and Niger, or with overpowering neighbours, such as Puerto Rico and Mongolia, or with debts that deliver them into the hands of creditors, such as Mauritania and Chile, have foreign policies which are dominated by outside structures, although they may not be totally determined by them.

Harold and Margaret Sprout have suggested that foreign policy-makers are not free agents, but neither is their behaviour wholly determined by external structures.[25] They suggest that there are a number of intermediate positions that can be taken up by observers, two of which are especially important. *Environmental probabilism* is a view that suggests that the environment makes certain kinds of outcomes likely to occur. Foreign policy-makers have an element of choice, but the structures within which policy operates are not, at least in the short term, either very manipulable or very sympathetic to the interests of policy-makers. *Cognitive behaviouralism*, on the other hand, sees policy-makers as having a greater freedom of choice to the extent that they can recognize it. But it is the understanding of a situation (the cognition) which effectively determines decision-making. However, when the decision is implemented, the 'real world' structures shape the outcome. These positions and the arguments that underpin them can be usefully summarized in a diagram which combines the three ranges of explanation: the spectrum between free will and determinism by the external environment; the spectrum between free choice and the cognitive environment; and the spectrum between cognitive and external determinism. *Figure 4.1* combines these three spectra in a triangle:

Figure 4.1

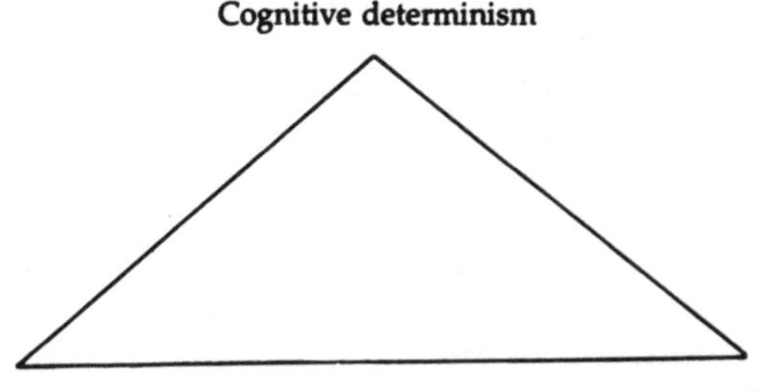

This triangle is helpful because it clarifies some complex arguments. No useful foreign policy theory, it can be argued, can be located at the apexes of the triangle. All theories must lie somewhere within the triangle, in the sense that they combine the three positions. Any theory which can be located on a line accepts a compromise between two positions while totally rejecting the position represented at the opposite point. This triangle does not, of course, explain anything, but it does help us to represent and classify the position which any foreign policy theory takes on the relationship between the environment and policy. It is particularly helpful when trying to make sense of the different ways in which the foreign policy literature attempts to deal with the problem of determinism.

DEVELOPING THE ENVIRONMENT-POLICY THEME

The intention of this final section is to suggest a way of thinking about the role of the environment in foreign policy processes which will be sophisticated enough to be worthwhile, simple enough to be usable, and based on the system framework which underpins this book. This section does not develop a new model, although there may be some new elements, such as the conception of a knowledge structure outlined earlier, which have not been widely used in foreign policy analysis.

Four important types of environment can be distinguished in much of the foreign policy literature. First, a security environment relates to the balance of power, to military security and to military force. There is also an institutional framework here, for the pursuit of security has led to the creation of a network of security alliances within which policy-makers operate. Second, the economic and financial environment encompassing structures of production, exchange and credit, provides another distinctive field of activity which constrains or at least affects foreign policy processes as well as forming the substance of some of the most important foreign policy problems. Third, knowledge and ideological structures, it has been argued, constitute an important field of activity which influence the foreign policy agenda, motivate policy, provide criteria for success or failure and establish a locus of power around which international negotiations or conflicts are organized. A fourth environment of policy is the domestic structure, culture and political system of the state on behalf of which the foreign policy system acts.

While there are important cross-currents between these four environments, they are conceptually separable, and other influences can be subsumed within them. Thus, for example, technology may be of great importance in foreign policy processes, but we do not need to argue that there is a separate technical structure. Technology can be seen as a part of the economic structure or, if it is military technology, as part of the security framework; alternatively, technology can be regarded as a facilitator of know-

Figure 4.2

	Psychological environment	Operational environment
Security		
Economics		
Knowledge		
Social structure		

ledge dissemination or control. Physical geography may also be a factor, but it does not need to be seen as a separate environment. It clearly plays a part in military security or the absence of it. It also provides resources, and contributes to the speed of change of knowledge structures. It may also shape domestic culture, political cohesion or disunity, and a sense of vulnerability or security in society.

These four categories of foreign policy environment provide a useful way of looking at the environment as a whole. Conceived as systems, the security, economic, knowledge and social systems can be seen as interacting with each other and with the foreign policy process in general. But, as argued in the first section of this chapter, each system can also be understood in terms of psychological and operational environments. This creates an analytical model which can be illustrated as in *Figure 4.2* in a matrix of eight boxes. This view of the environment of foreign policy can facilitate a structured and relatively sophisticated account as long as it is interpreted in a dynamic and interactive way. It is useful to consider how this framework might be used in a study of particular cases.

Canadian foreign policy, one might think, is relatively

straightforward. The country faces few immediate threats from the security environment, since the overall framework of United States strategic policy and NATO defence in the Atlantic provides a security system which satisfies the need for the defence of territory and of the political system. Internal structures, on the other hand, provide demands which are more difficult to satisfy. The Canadian population is largely crammed into a thin strip in the south of the country, while the society is deeply divided not only between French and English speakers, but also between east and west coasts and between urban and rural interests. The economy is strong by the standards of most countries; but the economy, and therefore living standards, depends on the activities of large companies, most of which are based in the United States. Canadian economic security, in other words, is largely beyond the control of Canadians. Furthermore, while Canadian natural resources are plentiful, the exploitation of them is largely in the hands of foreign companies. Climate, a limited population, a feeling of underdevelopment by comparison with the USA, and a lack of overseas interests, might all lead Canadians towards a rather introspective nationalism. This is indeed evident, but Canadians have also sought to articulate a set of interests outside any American-dominated structure of negotiation.

This combination of interests and historical circumstances helps to explain what might appear to be an odd feature of Canadian foreign policy. For Canada – or more accurately, the foreign policy élite in Canada – sees the Commonwealth as both useful and important. The Commonwealth framework enables Canadians to pursue certain economic interests while reflecting a broad social democratic interest in international cooperation and a domestic value consensus. The Commonwealth is outside the United States orbit, it embodies cooperation, and it does not cost a great deal either in financial or political terms. Thus on at least three occasions – during the 1956 Suez crisis; during the argument between Britain and the black commonwealth countries in 1970–71 over arms sales to South Africa; and over the question of economic sanctions against South Africa in 1985–87 – Canada played a leading role in seeking to manage differences between member governments so as to keep the Commonwealth going. No doubt if the costs of membership grow this picture might change. But over the last twenty years or so Canada has been perhaps the most enthusiastic member of the Commonwealth. This structure provides an opportunity for meeting economic goals and for asserting sovereign independence while fulfilling an important part of the national self-image.

Another case study which might be developed to test the utility of the framework would be changes in Irish foreign policy over the last thirty years or so. The Republic of Ireland was born in 1921 out of a struggle for independence from the United Kingdom. Even after independence, however, civil conflict continued, partly as a result of a domestic power struggle, partly over the question of whether or not to accept the partition of the North (Ulster) and partly over whether or not Ireland would retain some kind of constitutional relationship with Britain. After eventual withdrawal from the Commonwealth in 1949, Irish foreign policy in the 1950s and 1960s was very limited. Lack of resources and continued internal divisions gave little room for a domestic consensus on foreign policy to emerge. The Irish economy was wholly dependent on the British, while the Irish stance on security and political questions was marked by a determined neutrality. Attitudes which were in essence anti-British, pro-American and deeply Catholic, served to unite the Irish people and their rulers.

In 1961, however, the British application to join the European Community gave a shock to Irish foreign policy and stimulated a process of change which, in the 1970s and 1980s, led Ireland into a more active diplomacy. The stable, introspective, narrowly nationalist foreign policy of 'ourselves alone' was suddenly insufficient. If Britain joined the European Community Ireland would also have to join, and this would require a fundamental revision not just of the principles of foreign policy, but also of its organization, staffing and practice. More specifically, membership would transform the Irish economy. The market strength of the European Community threatened to overwhelm the limited and protected industrial development of the country, while Irish agriculture, then the largest employer (providing 60 per cent of all jobs), would be vulnerable to competition from more efficient producers, and would lose its main export market in Britain. Irish neutrality would also be at risk as soon as the Community started to develop a more coordinated foreign policy.

Fortunately for Ireland, General de Gaulle vetoed in 1963 the first British application to join the Community. This gave Irish policy-makers time to adapt to a fundamental change in their political and economic environment. While they had time to stimulate economic growth to some extent, the resource base and the economic structure were difficult to change. Attitudes and political structures had to change too. Industrialization in Ireland became intertwined with foreign policy in two ways: first as a means of creating a more competitive industry so that jobs and investment would survive EEC membership; second, because industrialization was international, Irish economic growth in the 1960s and 1970s was based on inward investment by foreign companies. This process of adaptation was successful to the extent that Irish dependence on agriculture for employment declined to about 40 per cent by the time that Ireland joined the Community in 1973 (and to about 25 per cent by the late 1980s). The role of foreign companies reduced the control that the Irish had over their own future, but made that future viable. Government officials and business leaders accepted the internationalization of the economy, although Irish labour organizations had more reservations. Preparations for membership were carefully planned and managed by government and industry.

Since 1973 Ireland has been able to adapt to Community membership because of the political and economic preparations which transformed the domestic environment. Dependence on the United Kingdom remains, but is diminished. The community has become a framework for the articulation of a much more active foreign policy than the introverted passivity which characterized Irish policy between the 1920s and the 1960s. This has involved a change in thinking, including a growing attachment to relatively free market ideas which form a main part of the current European knowledge structure, and a greater openness to international influences. A sense of 'being European' is important to the Irish élite not only because it implies 'not being British', but also because it reflects a break with tradition, a sense of modernization which has helped to focus loyalties at a time of fairly rapid change. The Community, rather than the links with either Britain or the United States, is now the main focus of Irish foreign policy. Irish leaders have found that the Community offers new scope for exercising their diplomatic skills, especially when Ireland holds the presidency of the Council of Ministers and they have the opportunity to represent the whole Community in international negotiations.

Thus changes in the policy environment which were initially a very unpleasant shock forced a re-evaluation of Irish foreign policy. This change in policy has with hindsight seen the emergence of a more confident Irish foreign policy, and a country more engaged with the outside world. Ireland remains neutral, but the conception of what that neutrality means in political terms has substantially changed. Ireland remains relatively poor by community standards, but changes in foreign political and economic policy have been successfully linked to a process of modernization at home which, over a generation, has brought dramatic changes to the economy and to the fabric of ideas which underpin policy.

The Canadian and Irish cases illustrate that the security, economic, knowledge and domestic environments do interact in ways which powerfully constrain all states, especially smaller or more marginal ones. But these examples also confirm that these structures do leave some room for choice; they create opportunities as well as threats which policy-makers may respond to positively, as long as they retain a domestic consensus and are allowed room for manoeuvre by the policies of the larger states.

CONCLUSION

Foreign policy is not made in a vacuum. As this chapter has argued, the environment within which policy is made and implemented provides both motives and context for action. The environment also offers opportunities and threats which shape policy, and a testing ground for the images and perceptions of policy-makers. It has been suggested here that foreign policy analysts like the Sprouts laid a valuable foundation for the study of the foreign policy environment. More recent work has gone some way to refine and qualify earlier findings, but the policy environment remains a relatively neglected part of the subject by comparison, for example, with the role of bureaucratic or cognitive structures. Five general conclusions can be offered.

First, the distinction between the psychological and operational environments of policy remains a useful analytical device which can clarify the basis of the working of the foreign policy system. Second, the traditional assumption of a boundary between domestic and international environments is much more problematic, especially with respect to economic issues, but it remains relevant in terms of law and constitutional practice. Shorn of ethnocentric distortions, the domestic structure can be seen as an important source of foreign policy. Third, foreign policy-making and policy management are political processes. The range of contexts within which policy is made do not directly determine policy; but neither are they filtered or mediated only through the psychological environment. They are also mediated by a political and social process within the foreign policy system. Fourth, this chapter has suggested a particular way of categorizing the environmental influences on policy, dividing the overall context into the security environment, the economic and financial environment, the knowledge and ideological environment, and the domestic structure. These are not the only possible categories but, taken together, they provide a useful and usable way of categorizing the context of foreign policy systems. Finally, it has been argued that the foreign policy analyst should see the relationship between policy-making, policy management and the environment as an interactive process which continually moulds and remoulds the behaviour of all the actors concerned. There is a process of continuous interchange between the environment and policy which is dynamic and complex.

NOTES

[1] See, for example, Snyder, R. C., Bruck, H. W. and Sapin, B., *Foreign Policy Decision-Making: An Approach to the Study of International Politics*, New York, Free Press, 1962; Sprout, H. and Sprout, M., *The Ecological Perspective on Human Affairs*, Princeton, NJ, Princeton University Press, 1965; Frankel, J., *The Making of Foreign Policy*, London, Oxford University Press, 1963; Modelski, G., *A Theory of Foreign Policy*, London, Praeger, 1962.
[2] Fitzgerald, C. P., *The Chinese View of their Place in the World*, Oxford, Oxford University Press, 1964.
[3] Paige, G. D., *The Korean Decision*, New York, Free Press, 1968.
[4] Wohlstetter, R., *Pearl Harbor: Warning and Decision*, Stanford, Calif., Stanford University Press, 1962.
[5] Janis, I. L., *Victims of Groupthink*, Boston, Houghton Mifflin, 1972; Shlaim, A., 'Crisis Decision-Making in Israel: the Lessons of October 1973' in Jones, P., *The International Yearbook of Foreign Policy Analysis*, vol. 2, London, Pall Mall, 1971, pp. 209–44; Lebow, R. N., 'Miscalculation in the South Atlantic: The Origin of the Falklands War', *Journal of Strategic Studies*, 6, 1, 1983, pp. 5–35. The role of psychological factors is considered in detail in Chapter 6.
[6] The theme of values and culture in policy-making is developed in a British context in Farrands, C., 'State, Society and Culture in British Foreign Policy' in Smith, M., Smith, S. and White, B. P., eds, *British Foreign Policy: Tradition, Change and Transformation*, London, Unwin Hyman, 1988, pp. 50–70.
[7] Smith, M. and Williams, P., 'The Conduct of Foreign Policy in Democratic and Authoritarian Regimes', *Yearbook of World Affairs 1976*, pp. 205–23.
[8] Shawcross, W., *Sideshow: Kissinger, Nixon and the Destruction of Cambodia*, London, Fontana, 1980.

[9] Vital, D., *The Inequality of States*, Oxford, Clarendon Press, 1967.
[10] East, M., 'Foreign Policy-Making in Small States', *Policy Sciences*, 4, 1972, pp. 491–508.
[11] See Clapham, C., ed., *Foreign Policy-Making in Developing States*, London, Saxon House, 1977.
[12] Morse, E. L., *Modernisation and the Transformation of International Relations*, New York, Free Press, 1976.
[13] Halliday, F., *Iran: Dictatorship and Development*, Harmondsworth, Penguin, 1979; Ramasani, K., 'The Iranian Revolution', *International Affairs*, 56, 3, Summer 1980, pp. 443–57.
[14] Mackinder, Sir H., *Democratic Ideals and Reality*, London, Longman, 1919; a useful recent discussion can be found in Garnett, J., *Commonsense and the Theory of International Relations*, London, Macmillan, pp. 55–60.
[15] Darby, P., *British Defence Policy East of Suez 1947–68*, Oxford, Oxford University Press, 1973.
[16] Yorke, V., 'Japan's Resource Diplomacy', *International Affairs*, 57, 3, Summer 1981, pp. 428–48.
[17] Bull, H., *The Anarchical Society*, London, Macmillan, 1977.
[18] Henkin, L., *How Nations Behave: Law and Foreign Policy*, 2nd edn, New York, Columbia University Press, 1979.
[19] East, M., op. cit.
[20] Strange, S., 'The International Knowledge Structure', paper presented to the Annual Conference of the British International Studies Association, University College of Wales, Aberystwyth, December 1987.
[21] Northedge, F. S., *The International Political System*, London, Faber, 1976.
[22] Hirschman, A. O., *National Power and the Structure of International Trade*, Berkeley, Calif., University of California Press, 1945.
[23] See Galtung, J., 'Structural Theory of Imperialism', *Journal of Peace Research*, 8, 1971, pp. 81–117; Frank, A. G., 'The Development of Underdevelopment, *Monthly Review*, September 1966, pp. 17–30. The best short collection of this school can be found in Smith, M., Little, R. and Shackleton, M., eds, *Perspectives on World Politics*, London, Croom Helm, 1981, Part 3.
[24] See, for example, Hill, C., 'The Credentials of Foreign Policy Analysis', *Millenium, Journal of International Studies*, 3, 2, Autumn 1974, pp. 148–65.
[25] Sprout, H. and M., op. cit.

5. Perspectives on the Foreign Policy System: Bureaucratic Politics Approaches

STEVE SMITH

This chapter is concerned with examining one perspective on the study of foreign policy behaviour which can be derived from the foreign policy system. This is the notion of bureaucratic politics developed in the 1970s by, among others, Graham Allison. There are two reasons for looking at this perspective. First it has attracted enormous attention in the foreign policy analysis literature. But, more importantly, it offers a way of explaining foreign policy decision-making that is distinctly different from the 'rational actor' account of the process. Whereas the vast bulk of writing on foreign policy behaviour has looked for explanations at the level of key decision-makers who are assumed to behave rationally, the bureaucratic politics account looks at the role of bureaucrats and the impact of organizational behaviour on the making and the implementation of decisions.

When bureaucratic politics was first formulated as Allison's second and third models in *Essence of Decision*, it appeared to pose a dramatic challenge to conventional ideas about foreign policy-making. Allison cast rational action as a monolithic process whereby the state behaved in a unitary way rather like an individual. Bureaucratic or organizational politics undermined this assumption by examining foreign policy as if it resulted from the interaction of individual bureaucrats playing political games to advance both their own and their organizations' interests. Such an apparently radical critique was bound to arouse considerable debate and many criticisms were levelled at both of Allison's alternative models. The first part of this chapter reviews the major criticisms that have been made. Partly in response to these criticisms, the two models were amalgamated and reformulated as one 'bureaucratic politics' perspective in later years. An examination of the bureaucratic politics debate also provides an opportunity to consider the generic problems associated with constructing theories of foreign policy. The second part of this chapter, therefore, follows the debate into the 1980s and discusses the way in which the bureaucratic politics perspective illustrates the problems of constructing foreign policy theory.

Bureaucratic politics was first established as an approach in the political science literature in the 1950s. It was developed and applied to foreign policy in the 1970s by writers such as Allison, Halperin, Destler, Steinbruner and Gallucci.[1] Of these, the work of Graham Allison has proved to be the most influential, with his case study on the Cuban missile crisis remaining a major study in the field.[2] This work provides an excellent illustration of the usefulness and also the limitations of approaches focused on the decision-making component of the foreign policy system. As such, the study is now summarized in many textbooks on international relations and virtually all monographs on foreign policy analysis.

At the beginning of *Essence of Decision*, Allison sets himself two tasks. First he attempts to examine the 'central puzzles' of the Cuban missile crisis. At first sight, it is argued, the events of the crisis appear deceptively simple. Despite warnings from the United States President about the consequences of so doing, and denials by the Soviet leadership that any offensive capabilities were being assembled, the Soviet Union installed a number of intermediate and medium range ballistic missiles in Cuba during the summer of 1962. 'Hard' evidence of the presence of the missiles was finally produced on 14 October during a mid-term election campaign in the United States. After lengthy discussions about possible courses of action President Kennedy ordered the placing of a naval blockade around Cuba, and this was announced, along with the first public confirmation of the presence of the missiles, on 22 October. By Wednesday, 24th, the blockade was in position. After some confusing correspondence between Kennedy and Khrushchev, the Soviet Union finally agreed to withdraw the missiles on 28 October. This agreement was secured in exchange for an American promise not to invade Cuba. Allison argues that there are three central questions which arise out of the crisis. Why did the Soviet Union put the missiles into Cuba? Why did the United States respond with a naval blockade? Why did the Soviet Union withdraw the missiles? These central puzzles, Allison argues, have not been satisfactorily answered, and his study attempts to provide more comprehensive answers.

The second, and perhaps the major task of Allison's study, is to illustrate the way in which different assumptions about foreign policy-making provide different answers to the questions raised, and even suggest which questions to ask. Thus, in addition to providing a more detailed and comprehensive study of the missile crisis, Allison is also concerned to offer solutions to the general problem of how to analyse foreign policy behaviour. He puts forward three propositions:

1. Professional analysts of foreign affairs (as well as ordinary laymen) think about problems of foreign and military policy in terms of largely implicit conceptual models that have significant consequences for the content of their thought.
2. Most analysts explain (and predict) the behaviour of national governments in terms of one basic conceptual

model, here entitled Rational Actor or 'Classical' Model (Model 1).

3. Two alternative conceptual models, here labelled an Organizational Process Model (Model 2) and a Governmental (Bureaucratic) Politics Model (Model 3), provide a base for improved explanations and predictions.[3]

Allison then proceeds to examine the three 'central questions' of the crisis in the light of his three models. The most important point to grasp about this analysis of the crisis is that Allison does not attempt to offer one correct version of it; rather, he is concerned to illustrate how three different approaches result in three different interpretations of the same events. As he puts it: 'the three accounts emphasized quite different factors in explaining the central puzzles of the crisis. The sources of the differences are the conceptual models each analyst employed.'[4] Yet, as he points out, while on one level the three models give alternative pictures of the same event, on another level they give different explanations of different events.[5] This is because each model emphasizes not only different features of the event, but also determines the rules of evidence, the choice of concepts, and the very way that the questions are formed. Allison is arguing, albeit implicitly, that the two alternative models he proposes are necessary for better explanations. Indeed he argues that if they are suitable in a case such as the missile crisis, which would seem to be an appropriate example for the application of 'rational actor' types of analysis, then the two alternative models would be of much more use in explaining routine decisions, where organizational and bureaucratic factors would have a greater impact.

CRITIQUES OF ALLISON'S ALTERNATIVE MODELS

Essence of Decision has attracted a great deal of attention since it was published. Much of this attention has been favourable, but there have been a number of critical commentaries.[6] Though bureaucratic politics has been utilized and developed in a variety of different ways, these commentaries constitute the core of a critique of Allison's models as originally formulated. They are reviewed here according to areas of criticism rather than by a summary of the content of each work. Six main areas of criticism can be identified.

The Alternative Models are not Original

Allison has been attacked by several critics on the grounds that his work is not original.[7] Although Allison offers Models 2 and 3 as alternatives to the more common Model 1, he has been accused of deriving these two models from the work of others. It has been argued that Model 2 is derived from theories of the firm and, as Wagner has noted, the application of theories of the firm to foreign policy behaviour may lead to serious problems; as he points out: 'What is a government bureaucracy's counterpart to the market, and how easy is it to transfer concepts and theories from one sort of enterprise to the other?'[8] In other words it is doubtful whether an approach derived from one area of human behaviour – that of the firm in the market – can be transferred to another very different area – that of foreign policy-making.

It has also been argued that Model 3 is very clearly derived from the work of earlier writers. Horelick, Johnson and Steinbruner maintain that the bureacratic politics approach is closely related to the work of 'Kremlinologists'.[9] A more common criticism is that it is based on the work of an earlier group of political scientists. Ball and Art each name the same four writers from whom, they argue, bureaucratic politics is derived – Schilling, Huntington, Neustadt and Hilsman.[10] Cornford even states that 'Model 3 . . . is pure Neustadt'.[11] Many have argued, therefore, that Allison's work is less innovative than he claimed.

It must be said, however, that Allison is clear in his acknowledgement of sources. He does point out that Models 2 and 3 are based upon the work of earlier writers;

in fact he spends some time summarizing the work of the authors noted above, indicating how they laid the foundations for the development of the two models.[12] As several writers have pointed out, Allison's originality lies in his use of previously disparate approaches in the analysis of one case study; as Cornford puts it: '(the) virtue of Allison's approach is that he makes the assumptions explicit, he applies them to a particular set of events, and he applies them consistently. He does not slide in the same account from one set of assumptions to another when the first set ceases to pay off.'[13]

Criticisms of his Account of the Cuban Missile Crisis

A more serious set of objections to Allison's work concerns his portrayal of the events of the Cuban missile crisis. Several writers have argued that his account of what happened is factually incorrect, which results in greater credence being given than is warranted to his argument that Models 2 and 3 explain critical aspects of the crisis. This dispute over the nature of the evidence has centred both on specific events and on a more general problem concerning the crisis. With regard to specific events there has, for example, been a debate over whether or not Kennedy knew that his previous orders to withdraw US missiles from Turkey had not been carried out by the time the crisis began;[14] over why there was a delay of ten days between the decision to make a U–2 photographic overflight of Cuba and the flight (which confirmed the presence of the missiles) actually taking place;[15] and over whether or not the US Navy fully obeyed Kennedy's orders that the blockade should be moved 300 miles closer to Cuba.[16]

While the debates over the events of the crisis are rather complex, and the evidence, in many cases, is not detailed or clear-cut enough to reach definite conclusions, there do seem to be strong indications that Allison has misrepresented the evidence. Certainly the facts of several key incidents may not have been as evident as Allison suggests. This is important not simply because he is presenting an account of the crisis, but it is especially significant because he bases the claim that his alternative models have better explanatory power on their ability to account for critical events of the crisis. In this respect the location of the blockade and the question of the US missiles in Turkey are test cases of Allison's alternative models. These two incidents are used by Allison to show that the standard operating procedures of bureaucracies can alter or even neutralize the impact of clear presidential instructions. If he was correct in his interpretation of these two events, then this would have supported the case for the development of his Model 2 (Organizational Process). The fact that he is seriously in error in presenting the two events detracts not only from his account of the crisis, but also from the theoretical utility of his alternative models.

If the facts concerning the missiles in Turkey and the location of the blockade do not support Allison's claims with respect to the explanatory power of Model 2, there is another question of evidence that relates more directly to Allison's Model 3 (Bureaucratic Politics). This concerns his use of the aphorism 'where you stand depends upon where you sit' to express the view that the stances adopted by the decision-makers in the crisis were a function of their bureaucratic positions. Some ten pages in *Essence of Decision* is spent outlining the relationship between decision-makers' bureaucratic positions and their policy recommendations. This relationship is the basis of Allison's bureaucratic politics model. Again critics have pointed out that this is not borne out by the record; claiming either that it did not happen like that, or that the aphorism demands too many qualifications to be applicable to the Cuban crisis.[17]

In some cases, such as the issue of whether the navy implemented the blockade as instructed, there is a straight dispute over empirical evidence; but in general this area of criticism involves degrees of emphasis. Allison is accused of presenting the evidence in overly dramatic terms which are very convenient to his argument. He has depicted, say his critics, a series of complex and confusing events as if they were neat and telling examples of the sort of puzzles that only organizational and bureaucratic politics models can explain. Caldwell has noted, for example, that bureaucratic politics models demand a quality and quantity of evidence that is rarely available and, given the ambiguity of what is available, analysts run the risk of imposing their theory on the data rather than testing their theory on it.[18] There is a clear problem with Allison's work in this context.

Criticisms of Allison's Portrayal of the United States Political System

Allison's account of the missile crisis has also been attacked for presenting an inaccurate portrayal of the US political system. This criticism has centred on two areas: his portrayal of the power of the President, and his treatment of forces outside the immediate decision-makers.

The power of the President

Several critics have argued, with considerable supporting evidence, that Allison's Model 3 underestimates the power of the president in that he treats him as one player among many.[19] As Krasner points out: 'leaders may find it advantageous to have others think of them as ineffectual rather than evil. But the facts are otherwise – particularly in foreign policy. There the choices – and the responsibility – rest squarely with the President.'[20] Although Allison spends much time illustrating how President Kennedy's choices were affected by bureaucratic and organizational considerations, his critics have argued that he consistently underestimates the ability of the President to get his own way. On the one hand this is because the ability of bureaucracies to establish independent policies or to avoid carrying out presidential orders (so-called 'slippage'), is a function of the President's attention and, thereby, of his values. Thus Steel has argued most forcefully that the debate among the President's senior advisers over the options available in response to the discovery of the Soviet missiles was primarily shaped by Kennedy's own values and preferences; having made his choice, he was able to utilize bureaucratic considerations to get his own way.[21] On the other hand the President establishes much of the bureaucratic structure which surrounds him in that he chooses the key personnel who, in the last resort, are responsible to him. Thus, while it is true that the President has to obtain information from, and discuss policy alternatives with, bureaucratic representatives, their freedom of action and their power is largely determined by the President himself. Presidential power, therefore, is much greater than Allison's analysis would suggest.

Allison's treatment of 'outside' political forces

A further criticism of Allison is that he fails to take account of the wider political system in the United States. According to Ball: 'Allison's governmental arena is too delimited; he fails to consider such non-bureaucratic elements of the American political system as, for example, electoral constraints and the power-political position of Congress.'[22] Thus Ball argues that the fact that the missile crisis coincided with mid-term congressional elections was of considerable importance to President Kennedy.[23] Allison seems to be fully aware of these considerations, however, and his discussion of the blockade decision contains many references to the congressional implications of various options.[24] A more salient criticism is that Allison's definition of politics is too narrow. As Perlmutter has argued: 'a theory of bureaucratic action explains the nature of the staff and its behaviour: it does not explain the direction and purpose of the political system'.[25] Couloumbis and Wolfe have suggested that Allison's work is open to the charge of ignoring the fact that American society is dominated by a business élite. They argue that the aphorism 'where you stand depends on where you sit' should be changed to 'where you sit depends on where you stand.'[26] This type of criticism might lead to a more extensive examination than Allison provides of questions such as why Cuba was so important to the United States.

The Criticism that Bureaucratic Politics Removes Responsibility

Allison's alternative models have been criticized on the important normative ground that they remove responsibility from government. By portraying foreign policy-making in terms of the 'pulling and hauling' of various non-elected bureaucratic groups, it becomes much easier for politicians to disclaim responsibility for policy outcomes. As Steel has argued most forcefully: 'where everyone is responsible for a decision, no one is responsible. If politics is the result of bargaining games among players, neither the President nor the nation can be held responsible for the decision made. If bureaucracies really run the show, what is the point of elections?'[27]

Krasner has also made this point:

> the contention that the Chief Executive is tramelled by the permanent government has disturbing implications for any effort to impute responsibility to public officials . . . if the bureaucratic machine escapes manipulation and direction even by the highest officials, then . . . elections are a farce . . . what sense to vote a man out of office when his successor, regardless of his values, will be trapped in the web of only incrementally mutable operating procedures?[28]

This criticism of Allison is only valid, of course, to the extent that the President is unable to get his wishes carried out, and this relates to the points made in the previous section. Nevertheless it does appear that the criticisms of Steel and Krasner are relevant to the extent that Allison tends to present the outcome of decision-making as bureaucratically determined and, thereby, does remove responsibility from the President.

The Criticism that Bureaucratic Politics Ignores Cognitive Factors

Several critics have argued that a concentration on bureaucratic and organizational factors breeds a tendency to ignore or discount the values held by the participants in the foreign policy process.[29] As indicated above, the degree to which bureaucratic factors can influence policy-making is, to a large extent, a function of presidential attention and, thereby, presidential values. Thus, as Art has noted, Allison 'undervalues the influence (or weight) of . . . generational mind-sets', since over many of the important issues and values there is no need for overt conflict as many of the key personnel share common generational perspectives.[30] On the other hand, as Krasner has pointed out, it is very tempting to see bureaucratic battles as reflecting bureaucratic differences *per se*:

> before the niceties of bureaucratic implementation are investigated, it is necessary to know what objectives are being sought. Objectives are ultimately a reflection of values, of beliefs concerning what man and society ought to be. The failure of the American government to take decisive action in a number of critical areas reflects not so much the inertia of a large bureaucratic machine as a confusion over values which afflicts the society in general and its leaders in particular. It is, in such circumstances, too comforting to attribute failure to organizational inertia.[31]

Thus differences which appear to reflect bureaucratic interests may, in fact, reflect wider disagreements over fundamental values. As Jervis has cogently observed:

> what seems to be a clash of bureaucratic interests and stands can often be more fruitfully viewed as a clash among values that are widely held in both society and the decision-makers' own minds . . . we have no grounds for claiming that a different constellation of bureaucratic interests and forces would have produced a different result.[32]

There does seem to be a serious problem here with the focus of Allison's models. As Ball has concluded on this issue: 'if United States policy is to be explained – or changed – the target is not the governmental structure but the values of American decision-makers'.[33]

Criticisms over the Extent to which Bureaucratic Politics is Applicable to Other Countries

While *Essence of Decision* is most detailed in its analysis of policy-making in the United States, it also attempts to explain Soviet foreign policy by using the same models. It is evident that Allison intends the two alternative models to be useful as tools for analyzing the foreign policies of other countries.[34] Nevertheless the applicability of his models to countries other than the United States has been questioned by several writers.

One group of writers has pointed out that Allison's models are of little use in analysing the foreign policy behaviour of developing states. Hill has noted that there exists 'a growing consensus . . . over the inapplicability of the insights of Allison, Halperin, Destler *et al*. to foreign policy-making inside less modernised states'.[35] Migdal suggests that 'these states do not . . . have enough stability of structure or form in their organizational routines or bargaining processes for the researcher to employ these conceptual models usefully'.[36] Brenner has noted that 'those features of national security policy-making accorded prominence in recent theorizing are not necessarily universal. They are more distinctive in the United States than elsewhere'.[37] Colin Gray, in his analysis of nuclear arms races, has argued that bureaucratic politics 'is really an Unruly Baronial view of the world, which may unfortunately prove to be more usefully analogical to England in the 1140s than it is to any capital in the world other than Washington DC'.[38] While these objections seem valid – since, in many cases, developing countries do not possess the bureaucratic structures necessary for these alternative approaches to be applicable – Weil utilized the approach in an analysis of North Vietnamese foreign policy and found it very useful.[39] Despite this example, however, it does seem clear that Allison's alternative models are of limited use in societies which do not have the same kind of political system as that found in the United States.

A serious criticism is raised by those writers who have argued that Allison's models do not even apply to the Soviet Union. Horelick *et al.*, Light, and Dawisha have all noted that, although Allison uses the models to analyse Soviet policy during the missile crisis, they are not strictly applicable to a country such as the Soviet Union.[40] In an excellent critique, Dawisha demonstrates that the bureaucracy in the Soviet Union is fundamentally different from its counterpart in the United States because of the pervasive influence of the Communist Party:

> [The] . . . role of the party in preventing bureaucratic conflict, the influence of ideology in providing universal goals, the representation of a wide range of functional and expert opinion, and the diversity of channels of access to the decision-making process all serve to undermine the applicability of the (Bureaucratic Politics) model.[41]

However several writers have argued more recently that the models do in fact apply to the Soviet Union. Valenta has argued that bureaucratic politics is of significant utility in explaining the Soviet decision to intervene in Czechoslovakia in 1968.[42] Indeed Valenta and Eidlin have written strong rejoinders to the Dawisha critique, with Valenta maintaining that: 'The bureaucratic politics paradigm can be one of the more useful tools for the analysis of Soviet foreign policy behaviour. Modified and tailored to the Soviet situation, it can substantially illuminate certain neglected aspects of the Soviet decision-making process.'[43]

In a West European context though, Wallace has argued that Allison's models are not relevant to an understanding of British foreign policy. As he puts it: 'Whitehall is not Washington; the open conflicts between sections of the administration which characterize bureaucratic politics in America have no exact parallel in Britain.'[44] A collection of essays on foreign policy-making in a number of West

European states examined the influence of bureaucratic politics on foreign policy and found it of little importance.[45] Wallace again, for example, after examining foreign policy-making in Britain, West Germany and France, concludes that 'in no case can the observer safely ascribe the outcome to bureaucratic politics alone'.[46] Faurby, having analysed foreign policy-making in Scandinavian countries, also notes that 'bureaucratic battles, however energetically fought, are not the main determinants of policy'.[47]

Wagner has offered a useful summary of this applicability problem. The particular context within which American bureaucratic politics takes place is quite peculiar, and this may account for the fact that bureaucratic politics is so important in the United States. Thus, the extension of Allison's models to other countries may be a less straightforward enterprise than he implies.[48]

GENERIC PROBLEMS IN THEORY CONSTRUCTION

Allison's work, although explicitly concerned with methodological issues, has also been strongly criticized for having serious flaws even in this respect. As an approach well-articulated at the time and much criticized since, bureaucratic politics offers a good example of the methodological problems confronting any attempt to construct theory in foreign policy. Many critics, for example, have argued that Allison is actually unfair to the rational actor model, describing it in more rigid and simplistic terms than it merits, thus favouring by contrast the subtleties of bureaucratic politics. Other criticisms can be usefully grouped into three.

The Relationship between the Three Models

One important criticism is that the three models are not easily separable; indeed Allison's later work has taken some account of this criticism in that he has merged

Models 2 and 3 to form a bureaucratic politics perspective which offers an alternative paradigm to the rational actor model.[49] However, at another level, Cornford has argued that the three models are based on one framework of social explanation – the rational choice paradigm: 'I do not believe that these models amount to incommensurable ways of seeing the world. It is not as though the three accounts had been written by St Augustine, Bentham and Mao Tse Tung. They bear a strong family likeness.'[50] Wagner again has summed up this problem by noting that:

> an effort to develop genuine models of foreign policy decision-making would most likely lead not to further development of Allison's three models but to quite different constructs . . . because Allison's three models are really just efforts to summarize the main features of three different bodies of literature. But since not much of that literature was written with the intention of developing formal theory, it would have been a quite unlikely coincidence that they should each provide the basis for three clearly distinct types of explanation of foreign policy decisions.[51]

The Logic–Politics Dichotomy

A related criticism also based on the separability problem is most forcefully stated by Freedman.[52] He argues that the apparent distinction between the three models can only be achieved by accepting what he calls the 'logic-politics dichotomy'. According to Freedman, Allison accepts this dichotomy in that he sees Models 1 and 3 as distinct and incompatible ways of viewing decision-making. Freedman, on the other hand, wants to argue that the two models lie at the ends of a continuum – at one end all is logic, at the other end all is politics – and that Allison adopts too narrow a definition of politics. Accordingly Model 1 deals with cases where agreed values are involved and no 'political' disputes occur, while Model 3 sees policy as the result of political battles over values and interests within the policy-making group. The essence of Freedman's argument is that this narrow definition of politics misses the crucial point that what is now contentious or non-contentious may be the result of past political disputes. Thus, at any particular time, the distinction between 'political' and 'logical' policy issues must not be seen as permanent: an issue may be deemed to be amenable to 'logical' analysis, in the absence of conflict, only because previous political battles have established the 'rules of the game' and have structured shared perceptions. Similarly, what is now a 'political' battle may not be so in the future and will involve varying conceptions of the 'national interest' which will, if successful, result in new areas of agreement and disagreement. Freedman concludes that: 'the structure and patterns can only be discerned by standing back from the immediate battles with a long-term rather than a short-term perspective, examining those things that the participants take for granted: the shared images, assumptions and beliefs and the "rules of the game".'[53]

It should be pointed out, however, that Allison does not see Model 1 as limited solely to non-contentious issues. By 'rational', he does not mean that the issues are clear and non-contentious but that they can be analysed in a certain way, that is, by tracing various conceptions of means—ends relationships. Nevertheless Freedman is surely right when he argues that what may seem to be a bureaucratic battle will involve various conceptions of the 'national interest', and therefore that Models 1 and 3 are not completely separable.

The Explanatory Status of the Models

A further criticism is that what Allison puts forward as his three 'conceptual models' do not actually provide explanations at all. Most critics would argue that a model is a construction of reality which either produces hypotheses which can be tested in some other way, or serves as a method of testing a hypothesis. In other words a model must contribute to the task of explanation by actually *saying* something which can be tested and assessed. Even false propositions help explanation as long as we can discover why they are false. A model, then, is required to make (or test) predictive propositions.[54] Allison, however, is not doing this. He is merely offering three different ways of looking at the same events. What he calls 'models' are really analogies.[55] We cannot assemble evidence either to prove or to refute them because they do not say anything; there are no predictive propositions to test, only alternative pictures of events. As analogies they can only identify factors that we might want to take into account. According to Bobrow, Allison is asking us to 'think about x (the Cuban missile crisis) as if it were a, b or c (rational policy, organizational process, bureaucratic politics)'.[56] Since one analogy is no more 'true' than another, we can only assess which analogy is the most useful. In one sense all three are true, and while this may be helpful it is not an explanation.

This point is made by Ernest Yanarella in the broader context of the philosophy of social science.[57] He sees Allison falling between two stools in terms of his contribution to a social scientific explanation. He is trying, on the one hand, to make some predictions from general laws (for instance, how individuals will react in a bureaucratic structure) but, on the other hand, he is only trying to show actions can be interpreted in a more *appropriate* or *intelligible* way (for instance, how the 'puzzling' aspects of the crisis are more understandable when viewed as examples of bureaucratic politics). This tension between two different purposes is typical, says Yanarella, of much modern foreign policy analysis. Certainly such criticisms do point to serious methodological problems with Allison's work.

THE CURRENT STATUS OF THE BUREAUCRATIC POLITICS PERSPECTIVE

Nearly twenty years after the publication of Allison's study of the Cuban missile crisis, it is evident that the development of thinking about bureaucratic politics has moved on. As noted earlier in this chapter, since Allison amalgamated his Models 2 and 3 in 1972, bureaucratic politics can be said to offer a perspective which is distinctly different to the rational actor account. We now have a general research perspective which focuses on the relationship between bureaucratic and organizational behaviour and foreign policy-making. The main thrust of more recent research has been to link bureaucratic politics to other theoretical perspectives which can be derived from the foreign policy system. After all, as discussed in Chapter 2, bureaucratic politics is only one of a number of possible perspectives and it is naturally rather tempting to think about how these might be linked. This is the motivation behind Barbara Kellerman's 1983 article on Allison's work.[58]

Kellerman picks up on the statement made by Allison in *Essence of Decision* that: 'additional paradigms focusing, for example, on individual cognitive processes, or the psychology of the central players, or the role of external groups, must be considered'.[59] Accordingly Kellerman proposes three more models, which she calls Models 4 (small-group process), 5 (dominant leader) and 6 (cognitive process). These three additional models each link work on bureaucratic politics with other perspectives on foreign policy behaviour. After applying them briefly to the Cuban missile crisis, she concludes that they collectively constitute a powerful explanatory device. The problem, however, remains that of deciding when each of the models is most likely to explain events, even though Kellerman offers a brief outline of which models might best explain which stages of the decision-making process during the crisis. The difficulty with her formulation of this linkage is that in all the stages of the decision, she sees several models as potentially useful for explaining events. Nor, of course, does outlining more models tell us anything about how the theoretical assumptions which underlie them are related. Robert Cutler has also discussed the linkages between bureaucratic politics and cognitive accounts of foreign policy decision-making, arguing that the two need to be brought together into some sort of cybernetic approach since he believes that the two are: 'respectively, the structural and behavioural aspects of the processing of information by persons'.[60]

A similar concern lies behind Jerel Rosati's revision of the bureaucratic politics model.[61] In his article he acknowledges that, although the model has been seen to have considerable explanatory power with respect to defence issues (see the work of Beard, Jeffries and Ciboski),[62] it does need to be linked with the wider literature on decision-making theory. Thus Rosati distinguishes between the structure and the process of decision-making and, following a case study of the SALT negotiations, he proposes a refinement of bureaucratic politics to make it one of three models of decision-making (the other two being 'Presidential Dominance' and 'Local Dominance'). The factor that determines which of the three models applies, according to Rosati, is the degree of involvement of the participants. What is particularly interesting about this formulation is Rosati's argument that the maxim 'where you stand depends on where you sit' is too much of a constraint on the bureaucratic politics model. By removing that element, however, the model loses most of its explanatory power.

If the general thrust of recent research on bureaucratic politics involves trying to see how it relates to other perspectives, the most important research question to be faced by those wishing to utilize this perspective concerns the issue raised above in connection with the work of Rosati. This is whether or not the strict injunction posed by Allison with respect to the influence of bureaucratic position on policy preference can be jettisoned. Rosati sees the assumption that 'where you stand depends on where you sit' as restricting the flexibility of the model, but it is precisely this relationship between position and preference that 'does the work' in Allison's conception of the bureaucratic model. Without it, there is only a very vague notion of linkage between position and preference, and quite how this can lead to theory is difficult to imagine. In other words, whereas in the original formulation Allison claimed that bureaucratic position determined policy preferences, to relax this injunction and to suggest that bureaucratic position merely has *some* impact on policy preference weakens the explanatory power of this model.

Having looked at the impact of bureaucratic position on US policy preferences during the Iranian hostage crisis, this author has argued that, although there was some relationship between position and preference, the strict linkage implied by Allison was unable to predict policy stances.[63] He concluded that the key relationship was between individual belief systems and the bureaucratic position of those individuals. In a later article with Martin Hollis, he developed this argument further by applying the notion of 'role'.[64] This notion implies that the actor has some freedom of choice whereas models that link policy preference to position imply that individual choice is determined by that position. Bureaucratic politics and the concept of role cannot easily be combined, therefore, and further work is required on the linkage between belief systems and bureaucratic position. The central dilemma is whether the deterministic model of bureaucratic politics can be modified without losing explanatory power, or whether the approach can be combined with one that sees the actor as being capable of choice, as in the notion of role.

CONCLUSION

Both Allison's work and other approaches, all of which have contributed to the development of a bureaucratic politics perspective, have been criticized and adapted over nearly two decades. Allison himself, as we have seen, has been criticized at empirical, normative and methodological levels. While he has to some extent been attacked unfairly, significant problems have been identified which do question the usefulness of his work. These criticisms, however, should not be taken as a wholesale rejection either of Allison's analysis of the Cuban crisis or of his theoretical contribution to foreign policy analysis.

With regard to his analysis of the crisis, *Essence of*

Decision remains the most penetrating and detailed account of the events. Although he has been criticized over certain specific pieces of evidence, the bulk of his analysis has been accepted by other writers. Allison's theoretical work, although challenged on several important points, has nevertheless made a lasting contribution to the study of foreign policy. Furthermore his work does have the crucial attribute of being open to evaluation: because of his self-conscious concern with methodology, he is explicit about his assumptions and the evidence he uses to support his arguments. Such an attribute is not only crucial, but is very rare in foreign policy analysis. Indeed, given a commitment to the cumulative nature of knowledge, such an attribute is a very important strongpoint of his work. On a theoretical level then, Allison's analysis of the Cuban missile crisis aids the quest for cumulative knowledge and the development of appropriate models of foreign policy behaviour.

A second qualification relates to the status of Allison's work within the general field of comparative foreign policy analysis. It is clear that the problems that have been identified in Allison's work are common to many, if not all, theoretical studies in foreign policy analysis. While the empirical problems are specific to this case study, the normative and methodological problems tell us something about the general problems of developing theoretical perspectives in the study of foreign policy. Thus, for example, the difficulty of applying Allison's models to other countries is a common criticism levelled at a number of other approaches. Similarly the methodological problems identified here are found, in varying mixes, in all theoretical perspectives on foreign policy. In other words, although Allison's work has been singled out in this chapter for critical examination, it should not be dismissed as an inappropriate way of explaining foreign policy behaviour.

Finally it should be stressed that Allison's work has been significant in a wider sense, to the extent that it has stimulated a variety of research endeavours within the bureaucratic politics perspective broadly conceived. Other work undertaken more recently has focused, for example, on the relationship between bureaucratic position and psychological preferences, or on how problems of communication within organizations affect bureaucratic behaviour. Thus foreign policy analysts should see this perspective in terms of other perspectives which have been articulated and developed in recent years. Two such perspectives are explored in the next two chapters.

NOTES

[1] Allison, G., 'Questions About the Arms Race: Who's Racing Whom? A Bureaucratic Perspective' in Pfaltzgraff, R. (ed.), *Contending Approaches to Arms Control*, Mass Lexington, 1974, pp. 31–72; 'Implementation Analysis: "the missing chapter" in Conventional Analysis. A Teaching Exercise' in Zeckhouser, *et al., Aldine Cost Benefit Annual*, Aldine, 1975, pp. 369–91; 'Military Capabilities and American Foreign Policy', *Annals of the American Academy of Political and Social Science*, 406, 1973, pp. 17–37. Allison, G. and Morris, F., 'Armaments and Arms Control: Exploring Determinants of Military Weapons', *Daedalus*, 104, 1975, pp. 99–130; Allison, G. and Szanton, P., *Remaking Foreign Policy*, New York, Basic Books, 1976; Allison G., 'Conceptual Models and the Cuban Missile Crisis', *American Political Science Review*, 63, 1969, pp. 689–718; *Essence of Decision*, Boston, Little, Brown, 1971. Halperin, M., *Bureaucratic Politics and Foreign Policy*, Washington, DC, Brookings, 1974; Halperin, M. and Kanter, A., 'Introduction' in their *Readings in American Foreign Policy*, Boston, Little, Brown, 1973, pp. 1–42; Halperin, M., 'Why Bureaucrats Play Games', *Foreign Policy*, 2, 1971, pp. 70–90; 'The Decision to Deploy the ABM', *World Politics*, 25, 1972, pp. 62–95; Allison, G. amd Halperin, M., 'Bureaucratic Politics: A Paradigm and Some Policy Implications' in Tanter, R. and Ullman, R., eds, *Theory and Policy in International Relations*, Princeton, NJ, Princeton University Press, 1972, pp. 40–79; Destler, I. M., *Presidents, Bureaucrats and Foreign Policy*, Princeton, NJ, Princeton University Press, 1972; Steinbruner, J., *The Cybernetic Theory of Decision*. Princeton, NJ, Princeton University Press, 1974; Gallucci, R., *Neither Peace Nor Honor*, Baltimore, Johns Hopkins, 1975.

[2] Allison, G. T., 'Conceptual Models and the Cuban Missile Crisis', op. cit,; and *Essence of Decision*, op cit.
[3] Allison, G. T., *Essence of Decision*, op. cit. pp. 3–4.
[4] ibid. p. 245.
[5] ibid. p. 251.
[6] There are many critiques of Allison which concentrate on specific problems; these will be referred to in the appropriate sections of the critique. There are, however, several critiques which make much more wide ranging comments about Allison's work; these major critical articles are: Art, R. J., 'Bureaucratic Politics and American Foreign Policy', *Policy Sciences*, 4, 1973, pp. 467–90; Ball, D., 'The Blind Men and the Elephant', *Australian Outlook*, 28, 1974, pp. 71–92; Caldwell, D., 'Bureaucratic Foreign Policy-making', *American Behavioural Scientist*, 21, 1977, pp. 87–110; Caldwell, D)., 'A Research Note on the Quarantine of Cuba', *International Studies Quarterly*, 22, 1978, pp. 625–33; Cornford, J. P., 'The Illusion of Decision', *British Journal of Political Science*, 4, 1974, pp. 231–43; Dawisha, K., 'The Limits of the Bureaucratic Politics Model: Observations on the Soviet Case', *Studies in Comparative Communism* vol. xiii (4), 1980, pp. 300–46; Freedman, L., 'Logic, Politics and Foreign Policy Processes', *International Affairs*, 52, 1976, pp. 434–49; Krasner, S. 'Are Bureaucracies Important? (or Allison Wonderland)', *Foreign Policy*, 7, 1972, pp. 159–79; Steel, R., 'Cooling It', *New York Review of Books*, 19 October 1972, pp. 43–6; Wagner, W. 'Dissolving the State: Three Recent Perspectives on International Relations', *International Organization*, 28, 1974, pp. 435–66.
[7] See, for example, Cornford, J, op. cit. p. 234.
[8]Wagner, W., op. cit. p. 450.
[9] Horelick, A., Johnson, A. and Steinbruner, J., *The Study of Soviet Foreign Policy: Decision–Theory–Related Approaches*, Beverley Hills, Calif., Sage, 1975, p. 55.
[10] Ball, D., op. cit. p. 71; Art, R., op. cit. pp. 468–72.
[11] Cornford, J., op. cit. p. 233.
[12] See Allison, *Essence of Decision*, op. cit. pp. 69–78, for Model 2's origins, and pp. 147–62 for Model 3's.
[13]Cornford, J., op. cit. p. 234.
[14] Hafner, D., 'Bureaucratic Politics and "those frigging missiles": JFK, Cuba and US Missiles in Turkey', *Orbis*, 21, 1977, pp. 307–33. Bernstein, B., ' The Cuban Missile Crisis : Trading the Jupiters in Turkey', *Political Science Quarterly*,vol. 95 (1), 1980,

pp. 97–125.

[15] See, for example, Krasner, S., op. cit. pp. 172–4.

[16] For a fuller account of these problems see Smith, S., 'Allison and the Cuban Missile Crisis: A Review of the Bureaucratic Politics Model of Foreign Policy Decision-making', *Millennium*, 9 (1) 1980; Caldwell, D., 'A Research Note on the Quarantine of Cuba'. op. cit.

[17] The major critics on this issue are Art, R., op cit. pp. 472–3; Ball. D., op. cit. p. 77; Krasner, S., op. cit. pp. 165–7.

[18] Caldwell, D., 'Bureaucratic Foreign Policy-making', op. cit. pp. 99–100.

[19] See Art, R., op. cit. pp. 477–80; Ball, D., op. cit. pp. 80–2; Krasner, op. cit. pp. 167–9; Kohl, W., 'The Nixon-Kissinger Foreign Policy System and US—European Relations', *World Politics*, 27, 1975, pp. 2–3; Spanier, J. and Uslaner, E., *How American Foreign Policy is Made*, New York, Praeger, 1974, pp. 103–31; Steel, op. cit. pp. 43–6.

[20] Krasner, S., op. cit. p. 169.

[21] Steel, R., op. cit. p. 45.

[22] Ball, D., op. cit. p. 79.

[23] ibid.

[24] Allison, G., *Essence of Decision*, op. cit. pp. 185–210.

[25] Perlmutter,A., 'The Presidential Political Center and Foreign Policy', *World Politics*, 27, 1974, pp. 87–106.

[26] Couloumbis, T. A. and Wolfe, J., *Introduction to International Relations*, Englewood Cliffs, NJ, Prentice-Hall, 1978, ch. 7.

[27] Steel, R., op. cit. p. 46.

[28] Krasner, op. cit. pp. 160–1.

[29] Art, R., op. cit. p. 486; Ball, D., op. cit. p. 92; Krasner, S., op. cit., p. 179; Jervis, R., *Perception and Misperception in International Politics*, Princeton, NJ, Princeton University Press, pp. 24–8.

[30] Art, R., op. cit. p. 486.

[31] Krasner, S., op. cit. p. 179.

[32] Jervis, R., op. cit. p. 28.

[33] Ball, D., op. cit. p. 92.

[34] Allison, G., *Essence of Decision*, op. cit. pp. 252–63.

[35] Hill, C., 'Theories of Foreign Policy-making for the Developing Countries' in Clapham, C., ed. *Foreign Policy-Making in Developing States*, Farnborough, Hants, Saxon House, 1978, p. 2.

[36] Migdal, J. S., 'International Structure and External Behaviour', *International Relations*, 1974, p. 519.

[37] Brenner, M. J., 'Bureaucratic Politics in Foreign Policy', *Armed Forces and Society*, 2, 1976, p. 332.
[38] Gray, C., 'How Does the Nuclear Arms Race Work?' *Cooperation and Conflict*, IX, 1974, p. 290.
[39] Weil, H., 'Can Bureaucracies be Rational Actors?' *International Studies Quarterly*, 19, 1975, p. 464.
[40] Horelick, A. *et al.*, op. cit. pp. 41–2: Dawisha, K., op.cit.; Light, M., 'Approaches to the Study of Soviet Foreign Policy', paper presented to National Association for Soviet and East European Studies Annual Conference, 1979, pp. 14–19.
[41] Dawisha, K., op. cit. p. 325.
[42] Valenta, J., *Soviet Intervention in Czechoslovakia, 1968: Anatomy of a Decision*, Baltimore, Johns Hopkins University Press, 1979; 'Soviet Decisionmaking in Czechoslovakia, 1968' in Valenta, J. and Potter, W., eds, *Soviet Decisionmaking for National Security*, London, Allen & Unwin, 1984, pp. 165–84; and 'The Bureaucratic Politics Paradigm and the Soviet Invasion of Czechoslovakia', *Political Science Quarterly*, 94 (1), 1979, pp. 55–76.
[43] Valenta, J., 'Czechoslovakia and Afghanistan: Comparative Comments'; and Eidlin, F., 'Comment', in *Studies in Comparative Communism*, vol. xiii (4), 1980, pp. 332–42 and 329–31. The quotation can be found on p. 332.
[44] Wallace, W., *The Foreign Policy Process in Britain*, London, Royal Institute of International Affairs, 1975, p. 9.
[45] Wallace, W. and Paterson, W., eds, *Foreign Policy-Making in Western Europe*, Farnborough, Hants., Saxon House, 1978.
[46] ibid. p. 48.
[47] ibid. p. 124.
[48] Wagner. H., op. cit. p. 451.
[49] See Allison, G. and Halperin, M., op. cit.
[50] Cornford. J., op. cit., p. 242.
[51] Wagner, H., op. cit. p. 451.
[52] Freedman, L., op. cit.
[53] ibid. p. 449.
[54] See Ball, D., op. cit. p. 88.
[55] Bobrow, D., *International Relations: New Approaches*. New York, Free Press, 1972, p. 41.
[56] Bobrow, D., 'The Relevance Potential of Different Products' in Tanter, R. and Ullman, R., eds, *Theory and Policy in International Relations*, op. cit. p. 206.
[57] Yanarella, E., ' "Reconstructed Logic" and "Logic-in-use" ' in

'Decision-making Analysis: Graham Allison', *Polity*, 8, 1975, pp. 156–72. See also Steiner, M., 'The Elusive Essence of Decision', *International Studies Quarterly* 21, 1977, pp. 389–422.

[58] Kellerman, B., 'Allison Redux: Three more decision-making models' *Polity*, 15 (3), 1983, pp. 351–67.

[59] Allison, G., *Essence of Decision*, op. cit. p. 277.

[60] Cutler, R., 'The Formation of Soviet Foreign Policy: Organizational and Cognitive Processes', *World Politics*, vol. XXXIV (3), 1982, pp. 418–36. The quotation can be found on p. 419.

[61] Rosati, J., 'Developing a Systematic Decision-making Framework: Bureaucratic Politics in Perspective', *World Politics*, vol. XXXIII (2), 1981, pp. 234–52.

[62] See, Beard, E., *Developing the ICBM: A Study in Bureaucratic Politics*, New York, Columbia University Press, 1976; Jeffries, C., 'Defense Decision-making in the Organizational-Bureaucratic Context' in Endicott, J. and Stafford, R., eds, *American Defense Policy*, 4th edn, Baltimore, Johns Hopkins University Press, 1977, pp. 227–39; Ciboski, K., 'The Bureaucratic Connection: Explaining the Skybolt Decision' in Endicott, J. and Stafford, R., op. cit. pp. 374–88.

[63] Smith, S., 'Policy Preferences and Bureaucratic Position: the case of the American hostage rescue mission', *International Affairs*, vol. 61 (1), 1985, pp. 9–26.

[64] Hollis, M. and Smith, S., 'Roles and Reasons in Foreign Policy Decision-making', *British Journal of Political Science*, vol. 16 (3), 1986, pp. 269–86.

6. Perspectives on the Foreign Policy System: Psychological Approaches

JOHN VOGLER

The application of insights derived from psychological research to foreign policy behaviour provides a second perspective on the operation of the foreign policy system. Chapter 1 makes it clear that one of the consequences of adopting a decision-making approach which focuses on the behaviour of the decision-makers themselves is that we must confront the difficult problem of how they perceive their environment. As Kenneth Boulding pointed out in one of the most influential books on the subject of perception, human behaviour depends on the image, or the subjective knowledge structure of an individual or organization.[1] The 'facts' of a situation never speak for themselves – they have to be selected, ordered and given meaning. An individual's environment contains so many stimuli, so much potential information, that to operate at all, he or she will require some mechanism to discriminate between what is or is not important and to give order and meaning to what would otherwise be a discordant jumble of sensory data. Psychologists have labelled the processes whereby this is achieved as *cognition*. Cognition thus involves those mental activities associated with acquiring, organizing and using knowledge. It is still very imperfectly understood, but theories have been developed, tested and then utilized in the study of politics and decision-making. The study of cognition is important for our purposes because it is in essence the study of what Boulding calls the image (psychologists might prefer to speak of an individual's cognitive system) and the ways in which it is formed, modified and operates, so as to structure perceptions and hence determine behaviour.

The idea that behaviour depends in part at least upon perception has been incorporated in the foreign policy literature since the 1950s. One of the earliest formulations was Sprout and Sprout's well-known distinction between the psychological and operational environments of the decision-maker, where: 'What matters in the process of policy-making is not conditions and events as they actually are (operational environment) but what the policy-maker imagines them to be (psychological environment).'[2] Equally a glance back at the first two chapters of this book will demonstrate how other writers have placed the decision-maker's image of the situation at the heart of their analyses.

The distinction between image and reality, between psychological and operational environments, would hardly matter if the two were always in correspondence. The point, of course, is that this is not so. Throughout recorded history the conduct of foreign policy has been bedevilled by examples of what appears to have been, with the benefit of hindsight, gross misperception. To put it another way, there has been a tendency for the images held by decision-makers to misrepresent their operational environment. Strictly, this must always be the case because an essential function of the image is to provide a simplification and ordering of the external environment such that it becomes both comprehensible and manageable. Yet there is all the difference in the world between the accurate and useful simplification one might find in a modern well-surveyed map and, for example, the kind of fantasies portrayed in medieval cartography. The latter, far from being useful, often contained the kind of misrepresentations that were positively dangerous if used as a basis for navigation. Some of the cognitive maps used by foreign policy decision-makers have been analogous to the latter and any student of modern international relations would not be hard pressed to find numerous salient examples with attendant disastrous consequences. Chamberlain's misunderstanding of Hitler's intentions, Eden's image of the Suez situation in 1956 and much US decision-making relating to Vietnam or, more recently, to the Iranian revolution, would all betray relatively severe misperception. In the early months of 1982 British intelligence was confronted with a stream of information that ought to have alerted them to the Argentine intention to invade the Falklands. Yet they managed to arrive at the wrong conclusions and to misrepresent the situation in a way that precluded timely deterrent action. Argentine perceptions of British intentions appear to have been equally divorced from reality.

This is not to say that such mismatches between image and reality always, or even usually, occur. It can, however, be argued convincingly that compared with other human activities, foreign policy is particularly prone to them. This is because decision-makers must operate in an environment that is not only highly complex and uncertain but which is also laden with threat and insecurity. The problem is compounded by the difficulties of communicating across cultural and linguistic boundaries where national self-images tend to draw sustenance from the portrayal of foreigners in a stereotyped and rather less than flattering light.[3] Although the frequency of misperception in foreign policy may be debated, what is much more certain is the gravity of the consequences when it does occur. In this respect a very substantial body of literature has been amassed which highlights the role of inadequate perception in deterrence, the escalation of crises and the onset of war. Political psychologists such as Ralph White have sought to explain East—West relations in terms of a pathological spiral of hostile and defensive misperception.[4]

It is one thing to establish the importance of perception but quite another to be able to analyse the images of decision-makers and to account for the way in which they are formed and modified. Clearly the most pertinent problem with which we need to grapple is the explanation of exactly how cognitive mechanisms operate to distort the psychological environment of decision-makers. The difficulties are more than evident. The essentially subjective nature of images makes them difficult to penetrate and describe. Psychological processes, and especially those of high policy-makers, are notoriously difficult to measure outside the controlled conditions of the psychologist's laboratory. The range of individual, group and social variables which may at first sight appear relevant is very wide indeed. Small wonder then that many analysts, while paying lip service to the significance of perception, have locked the psychological mechanisms of decision-making away in a 'black box' into which stimuli flow and from which responses somewhat mysteriously emerge.

None the less some innovative and thought-provoking investigations of the contents of the box have been conducted and it is the purpose of this chapter to provide a brief review and evaluation. In terms of the threefold classification of approaches outlined in Chapter 1, we may regard this work as falling within the third category in that the intention is to provide a particular perspective on the foreign policy system. In order to do this some analysts have attempted to penetrate the psychological environment by developing techniques which may be used to describe the images held by decision-makers. Notable in this regard are the 'operational code' and 'cognitive mapping' approaches pioneered by George and Axelrod respectively.[5] A second type of study reviewed in this chapter is explicitly concerned with the explanation of how such images process information. In particular, the problem of misperception is addressed in terms of psychological theories of cognitive dissonance and decisional conflict.[6] Finally, numerous studies have concentrated on so-called 'situational variables' focusing, above all, on the stress that is induced by crisis and the way in which this exacerbates perceptual tendencies towards over-simplification and closure to new information.[7]

When set in the broader context of the study of decision-making, such studies have sometimes been seen to constitute a distinctive 'cognitive approach' or even a 'cognitive revolution'. The point has been made that as well as providing a particular perspective, they also have important theoretical implications for the dominant paradigm of rational decision-making. Steinbruner and others have argued that cognitive theories can actually provide at least part of the basis for an alternative paradigm which poses a much more fundamental challenge to the rational model than bureaucratic politics approaches or the modifications proposed by theorists of 'bounded rationality'.[8] This debate is reviewed at the end of this chapter.

DESCRIPTIVE APPROACHES – OPERATIONAL CODE AND COGNITIVE MAPPING

Descriptive approaches attempt both to outline and to analyse the images of decision-makers and to trace the ways in which information is processed within the psychological environment. The most widely used technique has been *operational code analysis*. The original idea was proposed in Leite's 1951 study of the operational code of the Soviet Politburo.[9] It was reformulated by George in 1969 in a way that has provided the framework for all subsequent research.[10] As George admitted, however, the term 'operational code' is something of a misnomer because it does not actually denote a repertoire of immediate responses to particular problems. Rather it seeks to lay bare the general philosophical and instrumental architecture of an individual's belief system. Operational code analysis proceeds from a basic set of ten questions. Five of these concern philosophical beliefs or fundamental assumptions about political life. They concentrate on the following areas: is the political universe essentially one of conflict or harmony; what is the image of opponents; can history be controlled or predicted; is there optimism or pessimism concerning the achievement of political goals; and what is the role of chance? The remaining questions concern instrumental beliefs about the selection of goals, priorities, timing and the control of risks along with the utility and role of different means of advancing one's interests.

Since 1969 a large number of researchers have used these questions to outline the belief systems of various political leaders as diverse as Dean Rusk, Ramsay MacDonald and Mao Tse-tung.[11] Such research is mainly based upon combing documentary and memoir sources and the approach tends to be limited to those individuals who have extensively committed their thoughts to paper. Although beset by a number of theoretical and methodological difficulties, operational code analysis has the virtue that through adherence to a common set of questions instructive comparision of the belief systems of different politicians is possible.[12] An acid test of the validity of the approach would be if it were to be shown that its use could predict the responses of decision-makers to specified events.

In an interesting piece of research published in 1981, Stuart and Starr used the operational code approach to establish the general belief systems of Dulles, Kennedy and Kissinger, utilizing their writings in the period before they took office.[13] They then matched the operational code findings against a content analysis of the policy statements drawn from the periods when the three individuals were in government. The operational code analysis revealed that Dulles's perceptions of the Soviet Union were determined by an 'inherent bad faith model'. That is, whatever the Soviet leaders actually did, however conciliatory or cooperative their behaviour might appear Dulles interpreted it as evidence of duplicity and malign intent. As the authors noted, this was an example of 'closed information processing'. By contrast the images established for Kennedy and Kissinger were much more open and flexible.

The significant finding of the research was that the content analysis of verbal behaviour when each of the three subjects was in office produced results that would have been predicted by the operational code analysis. Dulles actually did respond negatively to variations in Soviet behaviour, while Kissinger and Kennedy exhibited the characteristics of 'open information processing'.

Cognitive mapping was developed by Axelrod and his associates during the 1970s.[14] Compared with operational coding, this is a much more complex and technically demanding enterprise. It too attempts to construct a model of the decision-maker's cognitive system. Whereas the method employed by operational code analysis is deductive, starting with a series of general propositions about key beliefs and fitting the particular characteristics of the subject to them, the cognitive mapping approach is inductive. The idea is to infer a cognitive map by studying the assertions and causal beliefs of the subject. The construction and analysis of such a map employs the mathematical techniques of graph theory and the map itself is composed of points which are concepts, linked by arrows which represent the causal connections made by the subject. The links may be positive or negative and the analyst having constructed the map will trace sequences of causal connections or 'paths' leading to various outcomes which are envisaged by the decision-maker to have greater or lesser utility. The maps themselves look very similar to the familiar flow charts used by computer programmers and systems analysts. Axelrod and his collaborators demonstrated how such maps could be drawn for a variety of individuals dealing with specific types of situation. This represents another difference from operational coding, which postulates a general and all-encompassing belief system. Essentially the map provides a guide to the internal logic processes of the decision-maker founded on the assumption that 'people do evaluate complex policy alternatives in terms of the consequences a particular choice would cause and ultimately what the sum of the effects would be'.[15]

Cognitive mapping can be used normatively to sharpen

decision-makers' awareness of their own mental processes, and Axelrod even suggests that they should be taught the technique in order to profit by drawing their own maps. But it is essentially a tool of empirical research. Experiments with cognitive maps led Axelrod to conclude that decision-makers tended towards simple causal thinking in their neglect of reciprocal causation and trade-off relationships. In other words favoured policy alternatives tended to be viewed as if they had no negative consequences, and vice versa.

Cognitive maps can be derived from documentary sources if these are sufficiently full, but are more easily constructed through the use of interview and simulation techniques. As with the operational code, an important test of the accuracy and usefulness of the technique lies in its predictive capability. Does the construction of an analytical model of a decision-maker's cognition allow a prediction of how a real situation will actually be perceived in the future? Shapiro and Bonham claimed success in this regard when they were able to use a cognitive map, drawn for an individual who was an expert in Middle Eastern affairs three years previously, to predict with some degree of accuracy his reaction to the 1970 Syrian intervention in Jordan.[16]

Despite these findings, both the approaches that have been considered here are essentially descriptive. They do not in themselves claim to explain anything or to test specific hypotheses. While their main function is to provide some insight into the latent structures of human cognition, they may be seen as laying some of the groundwork for the explanation of variations and aberrations in the cognitive performance of the decision-maker. Particularly significant is their demonstration of the way in which the psychological environment is often radically over-simplified and closed to new information. For an attempt to understand the circumstances in which such problems are likely to occur we may now turn to a number of explanatory approaches based upon psychological theory.

PSYCHOLOGICAL EXPLANATIONS – CONSISTENCY AND MOTIVATIONAL THEORIES

Instances of misperception are potentially explicable in terms of a range of psychological theories. There have, for example, been psychoanalytic studies of the peculiarities of particular decision-makers. Freud himself participated in a rather venomous study of Woodrow Wilson which attempted to explain the President's 'alienation from the world of reality' in terms of a deep-seated neurosis centring upon his ambivalent relationship with his father.[17] Figures like Hitler and Stalin have been grist to the mill of those wishing to establish the role of personality disorders in aberrant political perception and behaviour. As Russett and Starr note:

> All hark back to the classic formulation of Harold Lasswell – that there is a displacement of private motives on to public objects. Just as all people take out their emotional frustrations and personality quirks on the world around them . . . in this case decision-makers will also displace their private (idiosyncratic) personality drives on to the world around them – in this case, this world is also the world of diplomacy and foreign policy making.[18]

The problem is, of course, that such explanations are indeed idiosyncratic while 'the processes of misperception and selective perception are normal occurrences in normal people'.[19] In a thorough review of the literature, Sullivan concludes that although personality must have some impact upon foreign policy behaviour, it is very unclear as to exactly what kind of behaviour might be accounted for by such factors.[20]

Approaches based upon attention, learning and experience appear rather more fruitful. The concept of the 'evoked set' describes the quite commonplace observation that people are selectively attentive to information because they see what they expect or want to see and often react almost automatically.[21] One recent example that can be explained plausibly in these terms is provided by the experience of the British intelligence community in the months preceding the 1982 Falklands war. The Franks Commission Report marshalls evidence concerning intelligence assessments of Argentine intentions dating back to the mid-1960s and gives a quite unprecedented insight into the organization and operations of the Joint Intelligence Committee and intelligence assessment staffs.[22] What appears to have happened is that intelligence analysts evolved a 'stable mind set' or image of Argentine activity over a long period: Argentine diplomatic and military actions were to be interpreted as part of a lengthy strategy of graduated pressure in conjunction with negotiations and a sudden invasion was a possibility that could virtually be ruled out. This assessment appeared to be validated on a number of occasions which no doubt entrenched it even more firmly in the minds of the analysts. A number of well-publicized warnings of the possibility of Argentine attack in the first three months of 1982 were evidently ignored or discounted and right up to 31 March (the invasion occurred on 2 April), the existing image of Argentine intentions persisted in intelligence assessments. A number of factors contributed to this. The fear of the consequences of 'crying wolf' was certainly one factor. Also, as Franks noted:

> We are not sure that at all important times the assessments staff were fully aware of the weight of the Argentine press campaign in 1982 . . . they may have attached greater significance to the secret intelligence, which at that time was reassuring about the prospects of an early move to confrontation.

Not unreasonably the Report urges that in future the staff should be able to 'take into account both relevant diplomatic and political developments and foreign press treatment of sensitive political issues'.[23] This is treated as a problem of interdepartmental coordination in Whitehall, but a cognitive theorist might well identify a deeper failing indicative of the insidious influence of the 'evoked set'.

Decision-makers do not simply react in terms of their immediate concerns and experience. Certain 'formative events' in the past can have a powerful influence on creating the kind of stable images described by the operational code analysts. Misperception is likely to occur when images contain inappropriate historical analogies. The misuses of history have been discussed at length and frequent references have been made to the sway held by the Munich analogy over a whole generation of decision-makers.[24] Eden is often cited as a prime example because his statements at the time of the 1956 Suez débâcle indicate extensive use of outdated historical analogies. For him 'facing the dictators' in the late 1930s had been a formative experience because, unlike so many other British politicians, he had early arrived at a correct appreciation of Hitler and Mussolini's intentions. Unfortunately, as Prime Minister in 1956, he appears to have been convinced that he was fighting the same battle with Nasser over Suez where, in his own words, 'the pattern is familiar to us'.

The most widely accepted general explanation of cognitive closure, selective perception and the resilience of outworn images has been provided by the theory of cognitive consistency. This owes much to the work of Festinger on cognitive dissonance.[25] He postulated that there is an inbuilt need to maintain the consistency of the human cognitive system and that accordingly, psychological mechanisms function to avoid or reduce dissonance by screening out or systematically distorting information that might have a disruptive effect. In terms of decision-making this leads to what Jervis has called 'irrational consistency'.

As an illustration of what this means, we might consider the case of the smoker who has a government health warning printed on every packet of cigarettes and is frequently confronted with anti-smoking propaganda and health education campaigns of one kind or another. A decision-maker using rational procedures might be expected to take note of this dissonant information and reassess the costs and benefits of smoking in terms of the probability that health might be impaired with unfortunate consequences for self and family. In all likelihood the smoker would decide to give up. Yet, as any smoker can appreciate, such procedures are rarely adopted. Instead an irrational procedure may frequently be observed which serves to maintain 'peace of mind' or cognitive consistency while permitting the smoker to continue with the habit. There may be a refusal to link and order values such as health and the enjoyment of smoking or to comprehend the probability of certain outcomes – summed up by the common belief that 'it can't happen to me'. Pertinent information on the dangers of smoking may simply be ignored or distorted by inventing spurious reasons to question the validity of research into the effects of smoking. At the same time a set of rationalizations for the decision to continue smoking will be concocted. Incoming information, rather than altering the smoker's image, is assimilated into it. In the end, of course, the degree of dissonance may become so overwhelming that perceptual defence mechanisms can no longer cope. At this point cognitive consistency breaks down with a number of immediately distressing consequences of which smokers and ex-smokers are well aware.

In what is still probably the most influential book on psychological approaches to international relations, Jervis explores in some detail the application of consistency theory to the problems of perception in foreign policy, and with a wealth of supportive historical illustration.[26] The essential argument is that politicians and officials conducting foreign policy encounter similar problems and exhibit analogous responses to the smoker in our example. Decision-makers respond positively to information consistent with existing images and handle dissonance by selective perception and highly biased interpretation. They fail to make value trade-offs and indulge in 'post decisional rationalization' whereby beliefs are conveniently rearranged to provide justifications of behaviour. In effect the claim is that the consistency hypothesis can account for many of the cognitive phenomena or 'decision-making pathologies' described by operational code analysts and cognitive mappers.

The consistency hypothesis is not the only general explanation available. It has been challenged by an alternative 'motivational' hypothesis which attempts to explain the same observations of perceptual distortion in a rather different way and to provide more guidance as to when misperception is likely to occur. The fullest exposition of this approach as applied to decision-making is provided by the work of Janis and Mann.[27] For them the key to understanding is the fact that decision-makers are emotional beings: 'Among public officials who make major decisions affecting the fate of their country, we find a high degree of ego involvement in prior commitments, persistent longing for the gains they expect, and acute worry about the high costs and risks of intolerable losses.'[28] Their primary drive is not to maintain cognitive consistency but to reconcile the emotional conflicts that occur when decisions have to be taken. Janis and Mann thus present a 'conflict model of decision-making' which emphasizes the various patterns of 'coping' used to resolve decisional conflict or the 'simultaneous opposing tendencies within the individual to accept or reject a given course of action'.[29] Coping patterns are associated with cognitive processes of greater and lesser efficiency and receptivity to incoming information. This model is presented diagrammatically in *Figure 6.1*.

The model is constructed as a series of questions that decision-makers will ask themselves about the costs, risks and possibility of responding to a problem. If no serious risks are perceived at the outset, the response will be to do nothing (unconflicted inertia) or to make some form of incremental modification (unconflicted change). If neither of these responses is appropriate, the decision-maker may conclude that it is impossible to find a solution. This leads to a pattern of 'defensive avoidance' which can take any of three forms, procrastination, shifting the burden of responsibility to someone else, or 'bolstering' which is akin to the dissonance reduction mechanisms in cognitive consistency theory. Bolstering involves a search for the positive benefits of what was initially seen as an unsatisfactory course of action, coupled with a neglect of its negative aspects. This form of selective attention, along with procrastination and the denial of responsibility, serves to reduce the decision-maker's feelings of anxiety. If it is

Figure 6.1 **A conflict-theory model of decision making applicable to all consequential decisions**

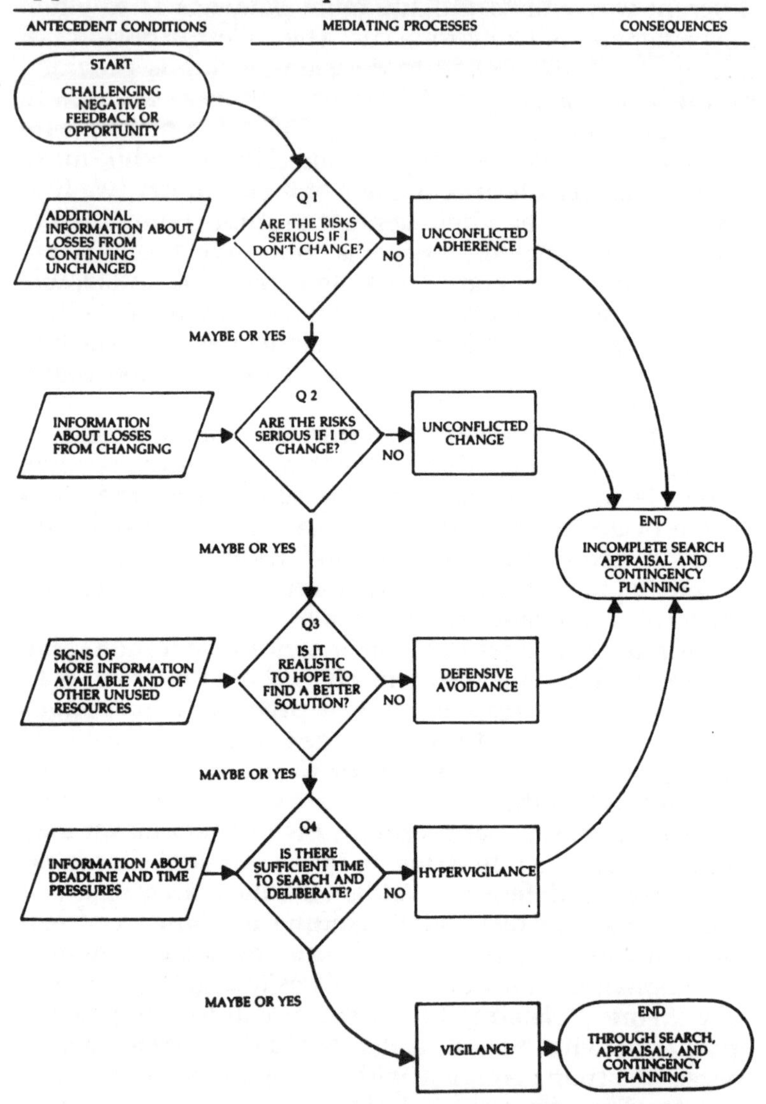

Source: Irving L. Janis and Leon Mann, *Decision Making: A Psychological Analysis of Conflict, Choice, and Commitment* (New York: Free Press, 1977) p. 70. Reprinted by permission of the publishers.

believed that there is a solution but the decision-maker is under extreme time pressure, the coping pattern will be one of 'hypervigilance' or, in more commonplace language, panic!

Janis and Mann argue that all four patterns lead to faulty information processing or 'incomplete search, appraisal and contingency planning'. The only coping pattern that approximates to the open and systematic treatment of information demanded by the rational model is 'vigilance'. Vigilant procedures involving thorough search and appraisal are only to be expected, however, if the decision-maker believes that the problem can be resolved and that sufficient time is available. The fundamental assumption of the model is that the answers to the sequence of questions will be determined by the decision-maker's search to find an exit that will ameliorate the stress induced by the decisional conflict.

Both the consistency and motivational hypotheses can provide valuable insights into the performance of foreign policy-makers. Consistency theory has been applied most widely, notably by Jervis, whereas Janis and Mann's references to foreign policy tend to be limited and spasmodic. On the other hand, according to its proponents, motivational theory has the advantage that it directly attempts to 'specify and explain the conditions under which people will be open to and will actively search for challenging information that could very well undermine their previous decisions'.[30]

Lebow has reviewed the utility of both hypotheses using a study of three crises: 1914; the Korean crisis of the early 1950s; and the Sino–Indian border crisis of the early 1960s. He reports that both hypotheses were 'extremely useful in helping to explain decision-making failures in three different cultural contexts. Employed together they offered more insight into these situations than either approach could have by itself'.[31] As to their relative merits, the motivational approach 'proved to be the most powerful analytic tool' because it alone 'provided a comprehensive explanation for perceptual distortion' while the consistency approach offered only partial explanations of the three cases.[32] In instances where both hypotheses could be applied, the motivational approach seemed to offer the more compelling explanation. In Lebow's view, the only conceivable way to settle the rival claims of the two would be to 'analyse the perceptual outcomes of a large number of cases in which expectations and perceived needs of decision-makers are in contradiction'.[33] However, the accomplishment of such a survey would probably be a substantial methodological feat directed towards an unnecessary goal, unnecessary because for purposes of practical analysis the two 'complement each other nicely by offering mutually supportive explanations. Advocates of either approach should recognise this important truth and refrain from attempts to denigrate or discredit one at the expense of the other. This, after all, would only be an exercise in irrational consistency.'[34]

THE CONTEXT OF PERCEPTION – CRISIS

A critical question in establishing the utility of theories about perception and decision-making failures is the identification of the circumstances in which particular types of misperception are likely to occur. A major criticism of Jervis's work is that although laying out many of the mechanisms and relating them to historical examples, he fails to provide an answer or to discuss the frequency with which decision-making pathologies are to be expected. Janis and Mann provide one answer in that the motivational model is specifically designed to accommodate the 'hot cognitions' that prevail under conditions of emergency decision-making. Much of the psychologically orientated writing about foreign policy has dealt with the investigation of crisis behaviour and, according to Oppenheim, it is this area of work that has exhibited 'the biggest and most clearly established gains'.[35] This is readily understandable in the light of the concern evoked in the practitioners of many disciplines by the connections between crisis and the onset of war in a nuclear age. Psychologists are no exception and they have had a special contribution to make, deriving from a tradition of laboratory research into the psychological effects of stress.

A well-established, although not universally accepted, definition of crisis has been provided by Hermann. Decisional situations may be classified in terms of three dimensions representing the perceptions of participants – threat, time and surprise. A crisis is said to exist when there is a serious threat to high priority goals, when the amount of time allowed for decision is sharply limited, and where precipitating events have been unanticipated.[36] A range of conditions have been observed in crises. They include a sudden rise in the volume of information that decision-makers are required to process (sometimes leading to overload); resort to informal channels of communication; and the location of responsibility for decision at the highest levels of the governmental hierarchy. When compounded by a sense of threat, an awareness of potentially devastating costs and risks, high levels of uncertainty and relentless time pressure – the result is to produce a psychological state of stress in the decision-maker. A great deal of highly suggestive work on the implications of stress for human cognitive performance has been presented in other, more accessible contexts: much of the work on international crisis represents a transfer of such findings and insights. The general psychological finding on response to stress is that the relationship between levels of stress and indicators of decision-making performance is curvilinear. That is to say that initially, and up to a certain level, stress can actually improve the performance of mental tasks but, as the level of stress increases, it leads to a 'progressive decline and disintegration of performance and ultimately panic'.[37] Research into stress reactions in crisis has generated a number of more specific findings. These include:

- increased rate of error;
- a tendency to aggression;
- diminished focus of attention and highly selective perceptions;
- a failure to distinguish between sense and nonsense;

- loss of ability to abstract;
- loss of complexity in the dimension of political cognition;
- reduction in the tolerance of ambiguity.[38]

Numerous case studies of actual international crises have confirmed the relationship between misperception and stress, with particular attention being devoted to the use of over-simplified, hostile stereotypes and the tendency towards 'tunnel vision' or an inability to perceive a range of alternative options and a fixation upon one, often military, solution. A test of the frequency with which information is likely to be misinterpreted in crisis situations is provided by Snyder and Diesing's quantitative study of fifteen such episodes. Their conclusion is that the chances of accurate perception are no better than four in ten.[39] Although misperception will not always occur in crisis, the literature leads strongly towards Janis and Mann's conclusion that the 'hot cognitions' associated with crisis-induced stress greatly exacerbate tendencies towards the various decision-making pathologies that have been discussed.[40]

A CRITICAL EVALUATION

So far we have been concerned with outlining the various psychological approaches and some supportive research findings as well as giving an indication of how they might be employed. It is now necessary to turn to some of the problems and criticisms that attend them. At the outset it is worth stating that the development of this line of investigation, from the early days of Boulding's 'image' and the Snyder, Bruck and Sapin model, has been impressive – particularly in terms of the identification of the cognitive conditions that give rise to misperception. The old criticism that psychological approaches lack economy and necessarily involve the study of a vast range of variables and a proliferation of 'boxes' between which relationships remain unspecified, looks increasingly tenuous. Yet a number of serious criticisms still remain unanswered.

Methodological Problems

The inherent difficulty of probing the latent structures and processes of the psychological environment has already been noted.[41] This has led some analysts to claim that the very attempt to do so is ill-founded and that the only rigorous method is to treat mental activity as a 'black box' and to deal exclusively with the measurement of observable stimuli and responses.[42] If this view is rejected, the researcher cannot avoid the problem of reconstructing something which cannot be directly observed. A common response is to make inferences from the writings and recollections of decision-makers. Such a procedure is open to a number of fairly obvious objections. Some of the very processes of 'post-decisional rationalization' that have been described and which one might wish to test, operate to distort the subject's representation of their own beliefs and thought patterns. The scope of research will tend to be limited, as the operational code approach has found, to prolific and articulate individuals like Henry Kissinger. Much relevant evidence, particularly internal government papers and records of policy discussions, is likely to be classified, 'shredded', or never to have existed on paper at all. Although systematic interviewing techniques, perhaps employed in the construction of cognitive maps, may provide a substitute, many decision-makers demonstrate an understandable disinclination to cooperate.

Historical cases may yield more extensive evidence and Jervis's work represents a substantial interweaving of such material with psychological theory. Yet this leaves the problem of generalizing from particular (and perhaps selectively perceived and documented) instances. Both contemporary and historical research may be rendered more systematic by the application of content analysis and related statistical tests, but these hardly command general approval and may sometimes only serve to impart a spurious quantitative rigour to highly unreliable data. Finally attempts to validate hypotheses by matching verbal behaviour (as in the Stuart and Starr study) must guard against the serious risk of circular argument.[43]

Many analysts, who are more than aware of such difficulties, have opted for research within a more controlled 'laboratory' environment. This can take the form of simulation (see, for example, Shapiro and Bonham) or the numerous psychological experiments that provide the empirical underpinnings of cognitive consistency and motivational theories. Janis and Mann's work, for example, is full of observations drawn from such diverse yet relatively accessible settings as anti-smoking clinics and the United States draft resistance movement. As critics never fail to point out, however, the use of results derived in this way to make deductions about foreign policy behaviour is a dangerous business. Clearly there are differences between senior politicians and bureaucrats on the one hand and hospital patients and simulation participants on the other. Indeed this may hold even if practising foreign policy-makers are invited to play in a simulation for there is a subtle change in context and role perception. Nevertheless it is a fundamental assumption of this kind of research that 'people are people' and that handled with care and due attention to dissimilarities the results may be valid.[44]

Explanatory Relevance

There is no consensus on this central question. Many have de-emphasized the role of psychological factors, often confining them to a residual category; whereas those involved in the study of psychological processes might assert with Shapiro and Bonham that: 'Beliefs of foreign policy-makers are central to the study of decision outputs and probably account for more variance than any other single factor.'[45] But there is only a limited understanding of the relationship between perception and behaviour and of the circumstances in which cognitive aberrations are likely to have a significant impact upon foreign policy. On a theoretical level, there is also a need to relate this type of explanation to the other perspectives discussed in this book and to explore whether it is possible to integrate them into a single explanatory framework.

Holsti has moved some way towards answering one of these questions by listing seven conditions under which the investigation of decision-makers' belief systems may prove rewarding. These include non-routine, ambiguous and unanticipated situations, conditions of stress and information overload, and decision-making at the apex of the governmental hierarchy.[46] In many ways this list reflects much of the work on crisis and aligns with the view put forward by Janis and Mann.

Perhaps the most telling attack on the relevance of psychological approaches concerns their concentration on the individual and his or her mental world. For many people the idea that explanation can be pitched at this level contains a fundamentally erroneous assumption about the significance of individuals in history. This raises the sort of question to which it is impossible to give a clear-cut answer. For example, how can we evaluate with any precision the importance of Dulles's operational code in the development of US foreign policy in the 1950s? Is it indeed sensible even to attempt such an evaluation when Dulles's views were moulded by his upbringing and environment? Images are not entirely personal or idiosyncratic, they occur within a social and ideological context. Thus, rather than debating the relative importance of individual and social factors, it is probably of more importance to trace the links between them. It is in this respect that the more recent work of Holsti and Rosenau on the foreign policy beliefs of a large sample of the American élite could be of significance.[47]

A similar point could be made in terms of the organizational setting of foreign policy. Policy-making is usually a collective process involving small group discussion, and Irving Janis has made a notable and very well-known contribution by analyzing the cognitive rigidities that are associated with the tendency to maintain consensus within a small group, whereby its members become 'victims of groupthink'.[48] As Boulding pointed out in 1956, a significant part of an individual's image is determined by the organization in which he or she works.[49] More recently Steinbruner has developed a cybernetic model of foreign policy-making which actually combines cognitive and organizational processes.[50] He argues that decisions are often taken in ways that are entirely alien to the rational model and which appear to reflect programmed cybernetic responses. In foreign policy one can speak of 'standard operating procedures' or the kind of phenomena dealt with by Allison's 'Model 2'. Steinbruner argues that cybernetic decision-making processes as encountered in everyday machines like thermostats require very simple discrete stimuli if they are to operate effectively. For instance, the humble thermostat works by measuring one simple variable in its environment — temperature — and making a simple programmed decision to respond by turning a boiler on or off.

Yet how can this provide an analogy for decisions taken by human beings who are confronted with an immensely complex and uncertain environment? Steinbruner's answer is that similar processes do occur. Programmed decisions and operating procedures within organizations are triggered by particular external stimuli. In order for this to happen the decision-maker, like the thermostat, must be able to concentrate very selectively on such stimuli and ignore most of the complications and uncertainties of the environment. This process of simplification and highly selective attention is, of course, exactly what has been observed by many of the cognitive theorists that we have discussed. The stable and simplified images of the world acquired by individuals in an organizational setting allow them to recognize and respond automatically to certain situations. Thus Steinbruner brings theories of cognition together with theories of organizational behaviour in order to explain how cybernetic processes operate in human decision-making. This cybernetic, or more properly cognitive-cybernetic, model is claimed to provide an explanation for decision-making behaviour that appears to be at variance with the rational model.

Whether or not Steinbruner's model is fully convincing, it illustrates the utility of combining cognitive and other organizational variables. It also suggests that attempting to compare, say, bureaucratic with cognitive explanations of foreign policy and to assert that one is superior to the other is not very fruitful. There are clearly ways in which each may inform and enrich the other and the need to relate psychological to other perspectives underlines once again the importance of using the organizing concept of a foreign policy system.

THEORETICAL COHERENCE – AN ALTERNATIVE PARADIGM?

Because the rational model has dominated the study of foreign policy decision-making, it is appropriate to conclude with some brief comment on the extent to which psychological approaches undercut rational assumptions and even provide in embryonic form the basis of an alternative paradigm. Such challenges are hardly unique to this area. As the last chapter makes clear, advocates of bureaucratic politics have mounted a similar attack from a different direction in their critique of Allison's 'Model 1.'[56] Steinbruner's cybernetic model provides an explicit alternative (although not a replacement) for what he labels the 'analytic paradigm'. The psychological case for modification or even abandonment of the rational model rests upon the assertion that studies of cognition demonstrate that human beings are incapable of fulfilling its rigorous assumptions. It will be recalled that rational decision-makers are assumed to be capable of making self-conscious choices concerning the relative value of their objectives, of perceiving new and pertinent information, and of formulating a range of alternative outcomes. Some of the work on the psychology of perception that has been described here casts a great deal of doubt on whether the mental processes which are actually observed in decision-making can ever measure up to these stringent requirements of formal rationality. Processes of selective perception and distortion operate to prevent the decision-maker acquiring a full range of pertinent information. When processing information 'irrational consistency' is imposed, trade-off relationships are systematically ignored and 'post-decisional rationalization' inverts the procedures that one might expect from a rational decision-maker. To use Janis and Mann's terminology, 'vigilant decision-making' tends to be the exception rather than the rule, especially under conditions of stress.

It is impossible to contradict the evidence that severe distortions can occur and that rational behaviour cannot be assumed. The study of the psychology of decision-making should alert us, not perhaps to the irrelevance of the rational model, but to the severe limitations that may be imposed by cognitive processes. Interestingly, both Axelrod and Janis and Mann are adherents to the rational model in the sense that they make a self-conscious effort to describe ways in which such problems may be overcome and the rational ideal more closely approached in decision-making practice. Thus, whatever the decision-making pathologies that have been found, the rational model appears to retain its normative status and indeed its position as the pivot of virtually all debate about decision-making.

Essentially, psychological or cognitive approaches lack the theoretical coherence to provide a realistic alternative. In surveying some of the literature, Kinder and Weiss put the point nicely: 'We see some emerging *descriptive* consensus about how the decision-making process looks, but little *theoretical* consensus about why it looks as it does.'[52] This is most evident in the rival explanations provided by cognitive consistency and motivational theorists. While this may not matter if the approaches are used only to provide partial insight into and explanation of particular foreign policy events, it most certainly matters if any attempt is made to erect some generalized model to supplant rationality.

NOTES

[1] Boulding, K. E., *The Image*, Ann Arbor, Michigan University Press, 1956.
[2] Sprout, H. and M., *Man—Milieu Relationship Hypotheses in the Context of International Politics*, Princeton, NJ, Center of International Studies, 1956.
[3] For a discussion of the special problems associated with information and knowledge in the international system, see Boulding, K. E., 'The Learning and Reality Testing Process in the International System' in Farell, J. C. and Smith, A. P., eds, *Image and Reality in World Politics*, New York, Columbia University Press, 1967, pp. 1–15. A standard summary of prevalent types of misperception is provided by Jervis, R., 'Hypotheses on Misperception' in Rosenau, J. N., ed., *International Politics and Foreign Policy: A Reader in Research and Theory*, New York, Free Press, 1969, pp. 239–54. See also Levy, J. S., 'Misperception and the Causes of War: Theoretical Linkages and Analytical Problems', *World Politics*, 36, 1, 1983, pp. 76–9.
[4] White, R. K., *Fearful Warriors: A Psychological Profile of US—Soviet Relations*, New York, Free Press, 1984.
[5] George, A. L., 'The "Operational Code": A Neglected Approach to the Study of Political Leaders and Decision-Making' *International Studies Quarterly*, 13, 1969, pp. 190–222; and 'The Causal Nexus Between Cognitive Beliefs and Decision-Making Behaviour: The Operational Code Belief System' in Falkowski, L. S., ed., *Psychological Models in International Politics*, Boulder, Westview, 1979, pp. 95–124; Axelrod, R., ed., *Structure of Decision: The Cognitive Maps of Elites*, Princeton, NJ, Princeton Univeristy Press, 1976.
[6] Jervis, R., *Perception and Misperception in International Politics*, Princeton, NJ, Princeton University Press, 1976; Janis, I. L. and Mann, L., *Decision Making: A Psychological Analysis of Conflict Choice and Commitment*, New York, Free Press, 1977.
[7] Hermann, C. F., ed., *International Crisis: Insights from Behavioural Research*, New York, Free Press, 1972; Holsti, O. R., *Crisis, Escalation, War*, Montreal, McGill/Queens University Press, 1972.
[8] Steinbruner, J. D., *The Cybernetic Theory of Decision*, Princeton, NJ, Princeton University Press, 1975.
[9] Leites, N., *The Operational Code of the Politburo*, New York,

McGraw-Hill, 1951.
[10] George, A. L., 1969, op. cit.
[11] A listing of the different studies along with an extensive bibliography is provided by Hopple, G. W., *Political Psychology and Biopolitics: Assessing and Predicting Elite Behaviour in Foreign Policy Crises*, Boulder, Westview, 1980, p. 53.
[12] A very useful critical review of the technique and a response by one of its foremost advocates is provided by Sjoblom, G., 'Some Problems of the Operational Code Approach'; and Holsti, O. R., 'The Operational Code Approach: Problems and Some Solutions', both in Jonsson, C., ed., *Cognitive Dynamics and International Politics*, London, Pinter, 1982, pp. 37–74, 75–90.
[13] Stuart, D. and Starr, H., 'The Inherent Bad Faith Model Reconsidered: Dulles, Kennedy and Kissinger', *Political Psychology*, 3, 3–4, 1981–82, pp. 1–33.
[14] Axelrod, op. cit.
[15] ibid. p. 5.
[16] See Shapiro, M. J. and Bonham, G. M., 'Cognitive Process and Foreign Policy Decision-Making', *International Studies Quarterly*, 17, 2, 1973, pp. 147–74; and 'Explanation of the Unexpected: The Syrian Intervention in Jordan 1970' in Axelrod, op. cit. ch. 7.
[17] Freud, S. and Bullitt, C., *Thomas Woodrow Wilson: A Psychological Study*, London, Weidenfeld & Nicolson, 1967.
[18] Russett, B. and Starr, H., *World Politics: The Menu for Choice*, San Francisco, W. H. Freeman, 1981, p. 310.
[19] ibid. p. 311.
[20] Sullivan, M. P., *International Relations: Theories and Evidence*, Englewood Cliffs, NJ, Prentice-Hall, 1976, pp. 26–40.
[21] See the discussion of the evoked set in Jervis, 1976, op. cit. pp. 203–16.
[22] *Falkland Islands Review, Report of a Committee of Privy Counsellors. Chairman: The Rt. Hon. The Lord Franks*, London, HMSO, 1983, Cmnd. 8787.
[23] ibid. p. 85.
[24] See the extensive comments on learning from history in Jervis, 1976, op. cit. pp. 216–87.
[25] Festinger, L., *A Theory of Cognitive Dissonance*, Stanford, Stanford University Press, 1957.
[26] See Jervis, 1976, op. cit. pp. 117–202.
[27] Janis and Mann, 1977, op. cit.

[28] ibid. p. 45.
[29] ibid. p. 46.
[30] ibid. p. 204.
[31] Lebow, R. N., *Between Peace and War: The Nature of International Crisis*, Baltimore, Johns Hopkins University Press, 1987, p. 224.
[32] ibid. p. 225.
[33] ibid. p. 227.
[34] ibid. p. 228.
[35] Oppenheim, A. N., 'Psychological Processes in World Society' in Banks, M., ed., *Conflict in World Society*, Brighton, Wheatsheaf, 1984, pp. 112–27, 115. This article briefly summarizes the existing research findings on the psychology of crisis. See also the same author's bibliographical review of the general literature, 'Psychological Aspects' in Light, M. and Groom, A. J. R., eds. *International Relations: A Handbook of Current Theory*, London, Pinter, 1985, pp. 201–13.
[36] Hermann, 1972, op. cit. p. 14.
[37] Oppenheim, 1984, op. cit. p. 115.
[38] These findings are summarized from Holsti, 1972, op. cit. ch. 1.
[39] Snyder, G. and Diesing, P., *Conflict Among Nations*, Princeton, NJ, Princeton University Press, 1977, pp. 317–39. Their finding is based on 272 messages and 330 interpretations. Misperception is also broken down into different categories; see ibid. p. 320, Tables 4–8.
[40] See Maoz, Z., 'The Decision to Raid Entebbe', *Journal of Conflict Resolution*, 25, 4, 1981, pp. 677–707, for a contrary case.
[41] A very useful summary of the arguments and problems is to be found in Holsti, O. R., 'Foreign Policy Makers Viewed Psychologically: "Cognitive Process" Approaches' in Rosenau, J. N., ed., *In Search of Global Patterns*, New York, Free Press, 1976, pp. 120–44.
[42] See for instance Singer, J. D., *A General System Taxonomy for Political Science*, NJ, General Learning Press, 1971, pp. 19–20, quoted in Holsti, 1976, op. cit. pp. 126–7, n. 16.
[43] The problem is discussed in Sjoblom, op. cit. pp. 40–5.
[44] Holsti, 1976, op. cit. p. 76, argues that this is an essentially empirical problem and the issue of scope should not be settled by a priori definitions of relevance.
[45] Shapiro and Bonham, op. cit. p. 161.

[46] Holsti, 1976, op. cit. p. 127.
[47] See Holsti, O. R. and Rosenau, J. N., *American Leadership in World Affairs: Vietnam and the Breakdown of Consensus*, Boston, Allen & Unwin, 1984; and 'Of Rifts and Drifts : A Symposium on Beliefs and Opinion and American Foreign Policy', *International Studies Quarterly*, 30, 4, 1986, pp. 373–485.
[48] See Janis, I. L., *Victims of Groupthink: A psychological study of foreign policy decisions and fiascoes*, Boston, Houghton Mifflin, 1972.
[49] Boulding, 1956, op. cit. pp. 27–8.
[50] See Steinbruner, J. D., op. cit., esp. ch. 4, pp. 88–139.
[51] For a critical view of such claims see Freedman, L., 'Logic, Politics and Foreign Policy Processes: A Critique of the Bureaucratic Politics Model', *International Affairs*, 52, 3, 1976, pp. 434–49.
[52] Kinder, D. R. and Weiss, J. A., 'In Lieu of Rationality: Psychological Perspectives on Foreign Policy Decision-Making', *Journal of Conflict Resolution*, 22, 4, 1978, pp. 707–35, p. 728. This article provides an excellent and thought provoking review of the implications for the rational model, in much greater depth than is possible here.

7. Perspectives on the Foreign Policy System: Implementation Approaches

MICHAEL CLARKE and STEVE SMITH

The last two chapters have dealt with foreign policy from specific perspectives derived from the general notion of the foreign policy system. This chapter introduces another way of thinking about the foreign policy system which raises different questions and highlights different issues. The perspectives considered earlier have focused to a large extent on the process of *making* decisions. This chapter concentrates instead on the process of *implementation,* seeing the ways in which decisions are implemented as a powerful tool for explaining foreign policy behaviour. This is to be distinguished from a focus which examines what the decision-makers involved intended that behaviour to be. The argument here is that viewing the foreign policy system from an implementation perspective not only offers an alternative set of insights into foreign policy behaviour, but also an alternative explanation of that behaviour. The chapter begins by briefly locating the process of implementation within the context of the foreign policy system. It then examines various patterns of implementation and highlights the importance of the processes involved in an explanation of foreign policy behaviour. A third section identifies the sort of questions that are raised by an implementation perspective before turning in a conclusion to a review of the theoretical implications of adopting such a perspective.

It must be stressed at the outset that foreign policy analysts have only recently begun to concentrate on the problems of implementation. This does not mean that they have ignored the process of implementing decisions, but they have been more concerned to focus on the decision-making process where, it has been assumed, the most interesting analytical questions are located.[1] The problems raised by an implementation perspective, however, are no less interesting or important than those concerned with decision-making. This can be illustrated by returning to our organizing scheme, the foreign policy system. When we characterize foreign policy as a system, we include in the system an 'output' and a 'feedback'. This refers to that part of the system where policies are put into practice, and where the outcome of those policies has an effect on the international environment which, in turn, feeds back into the policy machine as a new input. Thus the loop of the system is complete.

To illustrate, Britain's 'policy' towards South Africa during the Thatcher years has been to oppose the South African government's apartheid policy but to be reluctant to impose extensive sanctions on Pretoria. This may be a fair description of the stance that conservative politicians in the British government take towards the matter, but it is hardly an adequate explanation of the real output of the British foreign policy machine on the South African issue. For the real 'output' involves constant diplomatic dialogue with Britain's partners in the European Community and the Commonwealth, monitoring the economic and social contacts between Britain and South Africa, reconciling various interests between Britain and the front-line states, and between Britain and the USA, co-ordinating information on South Africa through various intelligence services, and not least, presenting all this in an acceptable form to public opinion and the media in Britain, where it represents a very sensitive political issue.

In other words as soon as we begin to apply the foreign policy system to real issues, both the importance and the complexity of what we call the 'output' and the 'feedback' components become very obvious. This is the focus of implementation, to ask the questions, how does the policy machine actually behave in the international environment, and what are the practical results of its operation? Any student of foreign policy who tackles particular issues soon becomes acutely aware of the fact that implementation matters. It matters in any number of different ways, but certain patterns emerge repeatedly.

PATTERNS OF IMPLEMENTATION

Slippage

The most common observation is that when the foreign policy analyst follows through a particular decision or series of decisions, it becomes clear that events are not happening in the way that the politicians who made the decisions either desired or expected. There is frequently some degree of 'slippage' between what decision-makers intend and what the policy machinery actually does in their name. Sometimes the slippage can be quite spectacular. In April 1980 President Carter launched a military rescue mission to try to free the US hostages held in Iran. He knew he was taking a major gamble; at best a finely calculated risk. But he could not have dreamt how badly wrong it would go.[2] The military simply proved incapable of doing what they felt they could do. Helicopters developed trouble and turned back from the mission; command procedures were inflexible; and at a critical juncture at the 'Desert One' refuelling stop a helicopter, with its rotor turning, got sucked into a dreadful collision with a tanker aircraft, with its engines running. In training, a helicopter and a tanker aircraft had never before been placed side by side with both sets of engines still running:

the down draught sucked the lighter aircraft into the side of the heavier one. The Iranians had done nothing to oppose the mission; at this stage they were unaware of it. The rescue attempt aborted itself through the failure of the military machine to carry through the logistics of the operation in ways that would normally be taken for granted.

Even when policies succeed, implementation failures can be remarkable. In October 1983 the US invaded the island of Grenada to deliver it from an unpleasant government that had seized power, and to counteract the influence of Cuba in its politics. A further rationale for the invasion was provided by the alleged danger to some 500 US medical students at the St George's University Medical School in Grenada. The invasion took the form of a major amphibious operation which swept the island from North and South, removed the government, and created a new interim administration. After all the military frustrations of the 1970s, it was an immensely popular act within the USA. Even within the realms of this resounding success, however, a study of the implementation of the military policy reveals a good deal of slippage.[3]

Over 3000 US servicemen could not fail to defeat a force of some 700 Cuban 'armed construction workers' and a small Grenadan army that tended towards instant desertion. Nevertheless US tactics were such that these forces were able to put up a surprising degree of resistance over more than three days. The US army was determined to prevent the navy and the marines from having all the action, and the Joint Chiefs of Staff pressurized the planners to include the 82nd Airborne Division in the invasion. But this Division was not capable of small independent, 'organic' actions. If it moves at all, it moves with a great deal of logistical back-up. Thus the 82nd Airborne introduced far too many ground troops on to the island and proceeded to move very slowly and cautiously forward, lacking any intelligence information — even accurate maps — of an island that anyone could have visited as a tourist only a week before. Meanwhile the navy's crack commando force, the Seals, failed to achieve their objective of silencing Radio Grenada because they attacked the wrong building; several of them were needlessly drowned in heavy seas. The army's crack Delta force also did not achieve its objective when it failed to capture Richmond Hill prison. The air force bombed the wrong target at one point and killed twenty-one inmates of a mental hospital, while the army had 9 per cent of its helicopters destroyed in action by an enemy with no anti-aircraft defences. This is not an impressive catalogue, though the whole operation will go down in history as a successful exercise of US military power in the pursuit of a foreign policy objective.

More typical examples of slippage occur in less dramatic situations. Foreign aid is a classic case.[4] Most governments allocate their aid budget with reference to certain implicit and explicit reasoning; more aid to the poorest, aid for ex-colonies or aid to democratic regimes under pressure. Such phrases embody the political thrust behind the policy. Very often, however, governments do little to follow up the allocation of aid funds. Once the money has been allocated and given to some agency or recipient government, then to all intents and purposes the policy has been implemented. But whether the aid has any real effect on the economy of the recipient state is a rather different matter. Food aid is often wasted because it sits on the dockside waiting to be distributed. Aid can be given in the form of lorries to do the distribution. But often they have short working lives as a perfectly repairable vehicle rusts in a compound for want of some spare parts which cannot be obtained. Aid can also be given on condition that it is spent on agricultural machinery to improve domestic farming, but this often runs up against local customs and practices. Machinery is often misused, misunderstood or left idle. In dire food crises feeding centres are established, but people leave the land to live near such centres and the local crops for the following year suffer as a result. Food aid is not, of course, the only type of aid activity but it illustrates the general problem very well. The allocation of aid funds may seem like the 'output' of the policy from the point of view of the political system in the donor country, but it is only the beginning of the real process whereby money has somehow to be converted into real benefits inside the recipient country. In the case of foreign aid, the slippage between intentions and reality is normally quite considerable, so much so that the rationale of aid policy itself is frequently questioned. The idea of slippage is the most obvious, and dramatic example of the way in which implementation relates to policy-making, and examples of extensive slippage always attract our attention. But this is not the only observable pattern.

Routine Complexity

A second typical pattern of outcomes in the implementation of policy can be described as that in which the implementation is not so much the outcome of the policy; rather it *is* the policy itself. This arises typically in cases where complex but routine behaviour forms the main impact of the policy. Where bureaucrats who work in a highly specialized field have to make important decisions on a day-to-day basis, diplomatic procedures and networks are established and there is a regular 'flow' of decision-making activity. In these cases what is normally called the policy – either by politicians or by observers – is little more than a rationalization of that which is being enacted from day to day: our policy is not what we choose; it is what we are doing. Clearly there are elements of this phenomenon in most policy areas. In many cases it is a significant element; in some cases it is the overwhelming reality of the situation.[5]

Good examples of this pattern arise in the realm of foreign economic policy. The government may have a policy in relation to the value of its currency and international exchange rates. But such a policy is normally expressed at a high level of abstraction – to 'maintain stable exchange rates' or to 'manage the problems of the dollar' or whatever. But the reality of this policy is such that the outcome in the international financial system is determined by the constant detailed exchange-rate adjustments made by central bankers. Of course politicians can, and frequently do, become personally involved in such policies. But such is the complexity of the system and the limitations under which any one country has to operate its exchange rate, that the principle still applies; the practical flow of events provides the framework within which policy has to be articulated. Politicians, or bankers, may consciously try to alter the flow in a certain direction – that is, their input to the policy – and perhaps they will succeed, but the flow goes on and it is that which constitutes the main explanation of the policy.

This pattern of implementation is much more subtle than the patterns of slippage referred to above.[6] For here we are concerned with a shadowy area where decision-makers may or may not make a difference to the flow of events; where perhaps they may only think that they do; and where observers will disagree as to whether the government's policy on, say, exchange rates, has any real meaning. Another example of these sorts of policy dilemmas is provided by Britain's policies towards the European Community (EEC). The three successive Conservative governments since 1979 have had general policy stances towards the EEC. They have gone into General Elections declaring that their policy was this or that. It is arguable, however, whether the Conservative government has ever had a policy, in the strict sense of the term, towards the EEC as an institution. On particular issues stances have been adopted. At Mrs Thatcher's second EEC summit in Dublin in 1980 she was personally committed to reforming the payments system, declaring that she 'wanted our money back', even 'my money back'.[7] The Thatcher governments have also taken very clear stances over such matters as further increases in agricultural surpluses or the enlargement of the Community. But EEC business is an intensive day to day affair and those parts of the British government which habitually deal with it do so on the basis of well-established routines that are at once both cross-departmental *and* cross-national. So, for the vast majority of EEC issues, British policy consists of the painstaking consensus-building activities of a network of officials from all twelve member states.[8] What Britain 'wants' is in most cases what officials think they can achieve; and in the absence of very active and decisive political involvement from the top, the 'policy' is the sum total of the routine. The implementers, for all practical purposes, are the policy-makers.

Self-implementation

A third observable pattern of policy implementation concerns those policies which, in effect, implement themselves.[9] Governments have 'policies' on many issues which they have no power or perhaps no intention of doing anything about. Governments take stances on issues simply for the sake of expressing their view; of being on the side of their respective angels. All governments would claim it as one of their policies to express abhorrence at human rights abuses, for example. Governments take different views as to whether they recognize the legitimacy of Kampuchea or Taiwan or Gibraltar. Once they have expressed their policy in a speech to the United Nations (UN), or in their legislature, or in an address by the leadership, the policy has been implemented. In other words only certain types of policy require implementation in the sense that something is supposed to happen as a result of policy being adopted. A great deal of the stuff of international relations revolves around abstractions and declarations. So much of foreign policy is declaratory that a high proportion of it may be regarded as 'self-implementing'. Governments are required to express policy in the UN on a series of issues in which they have no direct interest. Even in more specialized organizations such as the Organization of Petroleum Exporting Countries (OPEC) or the Organization for Economic Cooperation and Development (OECD), not all issues will be of tangible importance to all of the members.

This is not to say, however, that the abstractions of foreign policy are unimportant. They may be vital, since so much foreign reaction is essentially perceptual. The refusal of any other government in the world simply to say in 1976, 'we recognize the Bantu homeland of the Transkei as an independent state', effectively killed the South African government's homelands policy. The UN General Assembly vote of 1971 finally to admit Communist China to the organization was a fatal blow to Nationalist China from which it cannot recover, though the demise of that state has been protracted. Abstractions matter because perceptions matter; and a great deal of foreign policy is abstract in the sense that it is essentially self-implementing.

Other patterns of implementation may readily be conceived: implementation which is entirely procedural; implementation which is designed to be ineffective, lest we suffer the misfortune of having our political wishes granted; implementation which is tangible in one field but perceptual in another; implementation which is designed to pursue contradictory objectives in order to avoid the need for political choice; implementation which is simply incoherent. There are many possibilities.

It should also be evident from such illustrations that implementation draws from many of the perspectives outlined earlier in Chapter 2. It is partly about bureaucratic politics, formal political control, standard operating procedures, and so on. There is no theory of implementation as such. While it is possible to say that there are theories of crisis decision-making which postulate that individuals under pressure will tend to behave in certain ways, there is no counterpart in the realms of implementation. It is not a theory but a general perspective through which to view the whole process. In this sense it holds the same status as the other general perspectives outlined in Chapter 2. We have chosen to concentrate more on it here, however, partly because it is a neglected area of study, since most analysts concentrate on political decision-making; and also because it has a different and wider focus than concepts such as incremental decision-making, bureaucratic politics, and so on.

Implementation studies are not only concerned with the process of foreign policy-making: they represent the tangible link between foreign policy and the wider international relations of which they form a part. For implementation covers not only the *outputs* of the foreign policy system but also the *outcomes* of policy processes in the world outside the foreign policy machinery.[10] Outputs and outcomes are clearly not the same thing. An 'output' refers to whatever the foreign policy machine does in the world – make a statement or give aid, for example. An 'outcome' is what happens as a result of it – general condemnation of the statement, or relief to the sufferers of famine, for instance. It is important to be able to trace the link between policy outputs and policy outcomes; or else to be aware that in many cases a clear link is not traceable. If so, this in itself tells us something valuable about foreign policy in that context.

The task of an implementation perspective is to try to characterize outputs and outcomes satisfactorily and then to cast the dynamic processes of the foreign policy system in that light: what role do formal political decision-makers play in creating certain outputs; how much of the policy output and the real outcome is determined by standard operating procedures; how much of the policy output is directed to satisfying domestic or personal demands, and so on? In a sense, one is reversing the intuitive flow of the foreign policy system in order to work backwards from observable outcomes, to policy outputs, to those processes which seem to have directly created the outputs. In such a perspective, political involvement and leadership tend to emerge either as a direct but sporadic determinant or, more likely, as a constant but rather indirect low-key factor which monitors outputs more than it directs them. Having established, therefore, some idea of what constitutes policy implementation and how it relates to the foreign policy system, let us turn more precisely to those issues which are of major concern to the implementation perspective.

THE CONCERNS OF IMPLEMENTATION

Many of the chief concerns of an implementation perspective can be readily imagined. The bureaucratic structure of a foreign policy machine is one of the most obvious. For bureaucratic structures may limit what is possible, or else, if something is possible, what level of performance can be achieved. Many examples of policy implementation are drawn from US military ventures; some successful, some not. And one of the factors which proves consistently important is the fact that there is no combined defence staff. Joint military operations, therefore, always involve a high degree of interservice liaison – not all of it very effective. The fact that under the Key West Agreement of 1948 the army operates only helicopters up to 10 000 feet while the USAF operates everything else, and the Marine Corps and the navy operate all their own air assets, also tends to place limitations on the scope and effectiveness of US military ventures.

Equally the implementation of British policy in relation to the European Community concerns many essentially domestic ministries such as Agriculture, Fisheries and Food, the Department of Trade and Industry or the Department of the Environment. But the process is dominated by the Foreign and Commonwealth Office and the European Secretariat inside the Cabinet Office. Thus the way in which British policy is handled, what is regarded as realistic, what can be compromised and packaged, and so on, is crucially affected by this feature of the bureaucratic structure. To know what the DTI 'thinks' about a particular Community issue will not necessarily be an accurate guide to what will come out of the British policy machine; it has to be seen in the context of the views of officials in the Cabinet Office, in the FCO and in the British representation in Brussels, the UKREP office, through which it will be channelled.[11]

Less obvious than bureaucratic structure, however, but more important, is a concern with bureaucratic ethos. For the ethos of a policy machine will determine the style in which issues are handled, the enthusiasm with which some things will be pursued over others, the determination of implicit priorities. While it is possible to be precise about bureaucratic structures, a study of bureaucratic ethos cannot be more than impressionistic, though some impressive studies have been made under the rubric of 'bureaumetrics'.[12] To have a sense of the ethos is vital, however, since most bureaucratic structures can be seen as capable of coping, or capable of reform, or of readjustment or restructuring. But the quality of policy outputs is affected far more by bureaucratic ethos. Structural reforms may make little real difference if the ethos is hostile; or it might change but take several years as generations of officials evolve within the new structure. Alternatively structural reform may be unnecessary if the bureaucratic ethos is highly responsive to change and an existing structure evolves under the pressures of efficient bureaucratic action.

In this respect a key concern in the study of ethos lies in the concept of bureaucratic 'coalitions' as a way of getting something done. When policy-makers or officials want something other than routine to happen, the issuing of orders is not likely to be sufficient to achieve it. Even in military organizations simply pulling at the chain of command does not guarantee success, for military structures have as many divisions, private loyalties and subcultures as any other bureaucracy. The military may be a good bet for taking orders, but it is no better than anyone else at carrying them out.[13] So to get something done it will often be necessary to get one part of the organization, perhaps, to add another function to its workload; for another to make itself primarily responsible for the work in hand; for another to change the way it has been working for many years; and for another to stop doing something it has usually done. All of this may have to be done among agencies in different types of organization, as when the military has to work with civilian contractors, or when, say, governmental consular services have to work with travel agents or sporting bodies. Most important, someone has to bring such implementing coalitions into existence *and to hold them together over time*. This is no small task even within a relatively homogeneous structure; it can be almost impossible when it has to happen across different types of structure, still more so when it involves different and foreign organizations operating under separate norms, legal codes and national jurisdictions.[14] To understand implementing coalitions among bureaucrats, therefore, some appreciation of the intangible factors — their history, prejudices, self-esteem, style and all that goes to make up an 'ethos' — is essential to any explanation.

A third concern of implementation studies can be expressed as the problem of political control. How can politicians and key, formal, policy-makers ensure that what they understand to be the policy is consistent with what the process is actually producing? There is no obvious answer to this problem.[15] Leaders can take a personal interest and check and monitor official performance themselves. Or they can share the task with close and trusted advisers who are of the same mind. But even ignoring the way in which a multiplicity of other issues crowd in on decision-makers, the fact is that there are limits to any one individual's energy and comprehension. Leaders can only check up on officials who are at two, or perhaps three, removes from them. In most areas of policy which are not essentially self-implementing, the depth of personal involvement — from the top — will not be great. All leaders and key officials have to take a great deal on trust. In practice, politicians can and do make real impressions on implementing coalitions. They do so because they have the power to raise the salience of an issue, to create urgency — even crisis — by their interest. They can often have a great effect on the ethos which bureaucracies hold and which permeates their natural implementing coalitions. But such political involvement is almost always both sporadic and short-lived. It is another question whether or not the ethos resumes its previous form when direct political interest declines or is moved on to other urgent business.

So we should understand political control as a periodic or sometimes cyclical pattern of interest which interacts with the constant routines of the implementing agencies. The relationship will change over time according to circumstances. Reforming leaders such as President Reagan,

Mrs Thatcher and Mikhail Gorbachev have undoubtedly made an impact on their government bureaucracies. We might speculate, however, that the two-term Reagan did not make a major impact on the ethos of a generally decentralized foreign policy machine. Mrs Thatcher, over three terms, has certainly influenced the ethos of a characteristically centralized British foreign policy process; while Mr Gorbachev, with an unlimited term, has been making strenuous efforts not just to influence but to revolutionize the ethos of the Soviet policy process, whatever its characteristic structure. It is never less than an uphill struggle.

All arrangements have to be policed in some way. This can take many forms: physical policing, through the prevention of human activity; coercion, through the threat of some unpleasantness; blackmail, through the manipulation of others' well-being; bribery, through payment or reward in kind; or encouragement to conformity, through the reinforcement of values and appeals to culture and reason. In practice, a mixture of all of these ugly-sounding concepts is applied most of the time to police the workings of most organizations. Many government employees are physically policed because they can be prevented from visiting countries on the other side of the ideological divide; or they can be transferred out of departments or regions in which their presence is troublesome. They are coerced because they are recipients of official or organizational secrets and face the law or other disciplinary bodies if they do not keep them. They are blackmailed because bureaucratic disobedience will cause problems for other bureaucrats. They are bribed because they are paid for their work and promoted if they do it agreeably; they may be accorded social status and honours as part of the bribe. They are encouraged to conform because they like to be professional, they gain self-respect, they feel they are doing something useful and necessary in a civilized society. At this latter end of the spectrum, the ethos of the organization will tend to create a self-policing regime, where the appeal to values is a sufficient sanction to guarantee obedience and endeavour. Political decision-makers would like to influence bureaucratic organizations only by appeals to values and culture, but in reality this is almost impossible. As William Mackenzie pointed out in the 1970s, in a philosophical sense 'power', 'violence' and 'decision' all go together.[16]

A fourth area of concern in analyses of implementation is the intellectual relationship between policy and action. As we have pointed out, 'policy' has a number of overlapping and confusing interpretations. Decisions, as we saw in Chapter 2, come in all shapes and sizes. Only some decisions will be directly related to a discrete course of action. The US decision to go ahead with the attempt to rescue the hostages in Iran would be of this type. At the other extreme some decisions or expressions of policy will not have any direct relationship to action and may well not be designed to have any discernible outcome. In between these two extremes there is an enormous grey area of policy in which there is a conscious link between policy and action, but it may not be consistent, it may well cover several areas and types of action, it may be difficult to trace, and it will almost certainly change over time. Sanctions policies, for instance, fall squarely into this category. States often adopt economic sanctions against their sworn adversaries. Their motives for this policy are usually very mixed: to express moral abhorrence; to please domestic or international opinion; to hurt the adversary; to show solidarity with their friends and allies. Over time, however, sanctions policies tend to change. After a period of time they generally inconvenience, rather than hurt, the adversary; they develop loopholes; they are often conveniently ignored, and their rationale tends to concentrate more and more on the moral stance which they represent. They develop a propaganda value which far outweighs their coercive value.[17]

The student of implementation, therefore, must pay particular attention to the intellectual relationship between policy and action. It is important to understand what is, and what is not, expected to happen as the result of a declared policy. In particular, policy tends to be made up of a series of sequential decisions. As the old saying in

Whitehall goes; 'once is a cock-up, twice is a coincidence, three times and it's a policy'. As decisions build up into a policy, the intellectual relationship between policy and action will almost certainly change. As policies go forward, many lines of action may become impossible, or quite contradictory, or simply unimplementable. So while the rhetoric and presentation of a policy – even the motives behind it – may remain remarkably consistent over a period, it is quite possible that the policy-action relationship can be in a state of flux. The pronouncements of decision-makers can never be more than a general guide to the intellectual relationship between policy and action.

Lastly a major concern of this whole process is the need to characterize what has been called the 'complexity of joint action'. Most policies that require something to be done have to use a number of different agencies to achieve a result. Sometimes the agencies will all be part of the government. Most likely some of the necessary agencies will be outside the government sphere. Where several agencies are involved implementation becomes very complex and one particular action becomes contingent on another somewhere else in the network. In 1987 western powers moved cautiously and piecemeal towards a policy of defending friendly shipping in the Gulf in the midst of the Iraq–Iran 'tanker war'. But this took a great deal of time to emerge. The USA and France both acted unilaterally. Other powers, Britain included, sympathized but felt unable to move until other powers had been seen to do the same. All the powers involved in the Gulf had to establish their own logistical facilities before their forces could operate; quiet diplomacy proceeded between them in order to provide an appropriate political framework for the action. In the event a *de facto* western policy seems to have emerged in regard to the protection of shipping, but it was almost a year in process of articulation and construction.

More typically, foreign aid policy of all types involves an enormous complexity of joint action, for here the end result is normally supposed to be the production of goods and services in some way. Those who allocate the funds, the programme scrutineers, the aid officials, the development workers, the host government officials, the contractors, the local workers and the bankers, transport staffs and consultants who support the project, and many others, all form a series of networks through which action must pass, at the appropriate time, in the correct order, without loss of coherence and purpose. Not surprisingly, these conditions are frequently not met. As Pressman and Wildavsky have expressed it: 'There is less of a challenge in explaining why agreements break down years after they have been entered into than in discovering why it is so difficult to implement them at the time they are made.'[18]

The importance of understanding complexity in this context is that we do not need to look for opposition in the domestic or international environments to understand why policies do not succeed as they were intended. There is no shortage of opposition in international politics, but the sheer complexity of joint action – either national action in an international context or, increasingly, joint action in an interdependent context – is sufficient to explain why many policies fail, some partially succeed, and most are determined from the 'bottom up' by the flow of complicated implementation procedures.

Many writers on policy analysis have been greatly absorbed by the problems of understanding and analyzing complexity, and there are many good studies.[19] Curiously, most writers do not consider the international arena in this respect since they tend to make the implicit assumption that this arena is somehow qualitatively different. But this is mistaken. The international arena in reality is a mixture of national and international elements, and is becoming more so as interdependence becomes more prevalent. It is in this international arena that all the problems of complexity are seen at their starkest; where some agencies will be foreign and operate under their own rules and norms; where implementation coalitions are absolutely crucial to the process; where political control is at its most tenuous since there are few direct levers which policy-makers can use; where institutions and authority are far less important than predictable patterns of behaviour. The international arena, in other words, is a fascinating subject of study for anyone interested in the subtleties of implementation.

IMPLEMENTATION AND FOREIGN POLICY THEORY

Adopting an implementation perspective can affect the study of foreign policy behaviour considerably. As the previous sections of this chapter have indicated, real effects on foreign policy flow from the nature of the implementation process. It is not simply a matter of emphasis to say that implementation matters. Rather, it introduces a different perspective and hence a new way of thinking about foreign policy behaviour. It is necessary, therefore, to be aware of what effects such thinking has on our general explanations of foreign policy.

There are two main effects, one empirical and one theoretical. The empirical effects concern the importance of the implications of an implementation perspective for the wider world of international relations. Let us imagine a set of policy-makers attempting to respond, say, to the actions of the Soviet Union in placing its missiles in Cuba in the autumn of 1962. In order to begin to articulate a response, they first have to take a view of why the Soviets placed the missiles there in the first place. In fact the US decision-makers in the crisis proceeded in a very logical manner and drew up a list of reasons why the Soviets may have placed the missiles in Cuba. These included notions of a diverting trap (to get the US to attack Cuba so that the Soviet Union could take Berlin); a defensive measure (to protect Cuba from US intervention); an incident in cold war politics (to test US resolve); a bargaining chip (to remove US missiles from Turkey); and an attempt to bridge the missile gap (to counter the US lead in strategic missiles by placing shorter-range missiles nearer the US). In this situation the US decision-makers were trying to impute motives to the opposition. The most common way, in all situations, of doing this is for the decision-makers to work backwards from the sort of goal-formulation we have just outlined to see which one is most consistent with the action as observed: in this case the placing of missiles in Cuba. They tried to assess which goal was most consistent with Soviet behaviour, so as to be able to impute credible intentions to the adversary.

In doing this decision-makers are, in essence, making rational actor assumptions. They assume that behaviour is goal-directed and purposeful. They may, of course, have a shrewd idea that the opposition is in a state of confusion and is not acting purposefully. But to decision-makers who must assume the worst, and would like to believe that they themselves act purposefully, this can seem to be a dangerous assumption. There is an inherent human tendency to assume that the opposition knows exactly what it is doing. Decision-makers have little choice but to do this, and their concern will be to obtain the best intelligence information that they can and integrate it with their previous assessments of, for example, Soviet ideology, personality, and so on, to construct an explanation that makes other states' behaviour seem most logical and rational.

This is where an appreciation of implementation becomes crucial. The early part of this chapter has indicated that in many cases the behaviour of the state — its output — is not exactly what its decision-makers intended. Yet, of course, it is the behaviour of states to which the other states in the international world respond. Policy-makers simply cannot know how much of the behaviour they observe is due to the more rational processes of decision and how much is the result of the less rational processes of implementation. So it soon becomes apparent that the concept of implementation is important if we want to trace the dynamics of international relations. To the extent that behaviour results from implementation, then we have an important source of possible misperception as each side reacts to the other's behaviour as if it were goal-directed. The first effect which follows from the adoption of an implementation perspective, therefore, is that we have to think rather carefully about the impact of the implementation process on international relations in general. We are aware that a lot of foreign policy behaviour is not the result of a conscious decision by policy-makers. Yet the very necessity for decision-makers to impute intentions from behaviour means that to explain the complexities of international relations we need to look much more closely at the effects of the implementation process on the perspective they take on any given issue.

At the theoretical level it is clear that foreign policy thinking has tended to ignore the implementation perspective, concentrating instead on those cases where a process of decision can be more clearly outlined; implicitly assuming that it was these processes that were to be explained. Foreign policy analysis has essentially been an analysis of foreign policy decisions as if that was the necessary and sufficient explanation of foreign policy behaviour. While foreign policy decisions are obviously of key importance in explaining foreign policy behaviour, this chapter has indicated that what we take to be 'decision-making' should be interpreted widely, and that the whole process can be cast in an implementation perspective to illuminate different aspects of it. Existing theories of foreign policy, therefore, may be complete theories of decision-making, but any one of them can only be a partial theory of foreign policy behaviour.

In most traditional accounts, implementation has been treated as an epilogue, or even ignored altogether. Where it has been referred to, as in Allison's work on the organizational process model, there has been a tendency to discuss it only as a slippage from the original decision.[20] This implies that implementation should be seen as something which essentially flows from the decision-making process. In this chapter, however, we have outlined how implementation offers a perspective which looks at the whole foreign policy system in a different way. It asks different questions and suggests different answers.

For these reasons, it is clear that implementation matters in two separate, but related ways. It matters in an empirical sense because implementation, rather than deliberate choice, may be the major determinant of a state's behaviour, and it is behaviour that is observed by other states as a guide to their own actions. It matters theoretically because it highlights the way in which existing accounts are really only concerned with the explanation of decisions. An implementation perspective, therefore, helps to explain both foreign policy behaviour and the sets of interactions that combine to form the substance of international relations. As the perspective develops in the literature, it provides another way in which to understand more and richer facets of the real world of foreign policy.

NOTES

[1] It is no coincidence that the majority of works on foreign policy decision-making tend to concentrate on analyses of crises or of particular controversial decisions.
[2] See, Smith, S., 'The Hostage Rescue Mission' in Smith, S. and Clarke, M., eds, *Foreign Policy Implementation*, London, George Allen & Unwin, 1985; 'Policy Preferences and Bureaucratic Position: The Case of the American Hostage Rescue Mission', *International Affairs*, 61 (1), 1985, pp. 9–26.
[3] *Christian Science Monitor*, 14–20 April 1984; *International Herald Tribune*, 30 January 1984; *Daily Telegraph*, 7 April 1984. For a general source see Thorndike, T., *Grenada: Politics, Economics and Society*, London, Pinter, 1985, pp. 138–75.
[4] See, for example, Pressman, J. L. and Wildavsky, A. B., *Implementation*, Berkeley, Calif., University of California Press, 1973, pp. 136–46; White, J., *The Politics of Foreign Aid*, London, Bodley Head, 1976.
[5] See a good series of case studies in Lewis, D. and Wallace, H., eds, *Policies into Practice*, London, Heinemann, 1984. See also Smith and Clarke, op. cit.
[6] Many of these shadowy problems are discussed in Hood, C., *The Limits of Administration*, London, Wiley, 1976. See also Dunsire, A., *Control in a Bureaucracy*, Oxford, Martin Robertson, 1978.
[7] Riddell, P., *The Thatcher Government*, Oxford, Basil Blackwell, 1985, pp. 207, 212.
[8] Clarke, M., *British Foreign Policy and the State in the 1990s*, forthcoming, ch. 3.
[9] The concept of self-implementing decisions was first developed by Hood, op. cit.

[10] See Dunsire, A., *Implementation in a Bureaucracy*, Oxford, Martin Robertson, 1978.
[11] See for example, Wallace, H., 'The British Presidency of the EC Council of Ministers: the Opportunity to Persuade', *International Affairs*, 62 (4), 1986, pp. 583–99.
[12] Hood, C. and Dunsire, A., *Bureaumetrics*, Farnborough, Hants, Gower, 1981.
[13] To appreciate some of the subcultures of military structures see Keegan, J., *The Face of Battle*, Harmondsworth, Penguin, 1978; Dixon, N. F., *On the Psychology of Military Incompetence*, London, Futura, 1976; Keegan, J., *Six Armies in Normandy*, Harmondsworth, Penguin, 1983.
[14] Excellent examples of this are provided by the gradual development of European Political Cooperation. See Hill, C., ed., *National Foreign Policies and European Political Cooperation*, London, George Allen & Unwin, 1983; Pinder, J. and Wallace, W., 'The Community as a Framework for British External Relations' in Wallace, W., ed., *Britain in Europe*, London, Heinemann, 1980; Wallace, W., 'Political Cooperation: Integration through Intergovernmentalism' in Wallace, H., Wallace, W. and Webb, C., eds, *Policy-making in the European Communities*, 2nd edn, London, Wiley, 1983, pp. 373–402.
[15] On the limitations of political control see Halperin, M., *Bureaucratic Politics and Foreign Policy*, Washington, DC, Brookings Institution, 1974.
[16] Mackenzie, W. J. M., *Power, Violence, Decision*, Harmondsworth, Penguin, 1975.
[17] Schreiber, A. P., 'Economic Coercion as an Instrument of Foreign Policy', *World Politics*, 25 (3), 1973, pp. 387–413; see also White, B., 'Britain and the Implementation of Oil Sanctions against Rhodesia' in Smith and Clarke, op. cit. pp. 33–51.
[18] Pressman and Wildavsky, op. cit., p. 92.
[19] Interesting summaries of the understanding of complexity in the domestic environment can be found in Anderson, J. E., *Public Policy-Making*, New York, Holt, Reinhart and Winston, 1979; Jenkins, W. I., *Policy Analysis*, Oxford, Martin Robertson, 1978.
[20] See esp. Allison, G. T. and Szanton, P., *Remaking Foreign Policy: The Organizational Connection*, New York, Basic Books, 1977, ch. 1.

8. Comparing Foreign Policy Systems: Problems, Processes and Performance

MICHAEL SMITH

An important theme underlying the earlier chapters of this book has been that of comparison between foreign policies. In discussing foreign policy decision-making it is almost inevitable that comparison will take place, either of one country with another or of one set of decisions against others. Likewise the argument that foreign policy can be conceptualized as a system of action invites the comparison of different foreign policy systems, while the focus on foreign policy as a set of interactions – either within governments or between governments and the outside world – implicitly raises the possibility of significant variations or similarities between national experiences. The impact of bureaucratic processes, of individual or group perceptions, or of the implementation of policy itself, has in many instances a comparative dimension, encompassing either different processes or different outcomes across countries or issues. In this chapter the aim is to make the question of comparison explicit and central, and thus to build on the material provided earlier while raising a number of new questions.

APPROACHES TO COMPARISON

In some essential respects foreign policy analysis can be seen as a particular manifestation of problems which occur for all social sciences, and which thereby create an important role for comparative study. Much of the promise of the social sciences throughout their development has lain in their apparent utility not only as a source of understanding but also as a guide to action. On the other hand a central problem for the scientific approach to society arises from the fact that its subject matter relates to matters of values, subjectivity and individual or group preferences as well as to political action. In terms of foreign policy, the promise is well expressed by Wolfram Hanrieder:

> Hardly any important topic of enquiry, empirical or normative, is not somehow connected with the constant ebb and flow of interactions between a political actor and the elements of the environment. To talk about the connection between internal and external politics means to talk about all the major elements that form the patterns of power and purpose in the domestic as well as the international system.[1]

So much for the promise: but it is clear that in stating the attractions of the enterprise, Hanrieder is also stating the difficulties. Many of the relationships and interactions to which he refers are complex, intangible or inaccessible, and the definition he uses is so broad as to make foreign policy potentially all-encompassing. One way of tackling the difficulties, and of developing a searching and focused analysis, is to adopt criteria and methods of comparison. The comparative approach can assist greatly in the evaluation of events, by providing some measure of their general significance and of the variations to which they are subject. This is not to deny that there are dangers in comparison, created by the complexity, intangibility and inaccessibility of foreign policy action; rather, it is to claim that structured and focused attempts to compare foreign policy systems can provide insights and evidence which might not be forthcoming from more limited studies.

If the general utility of comparison is established, what might be its more specific uses? Michael Hass has identified four interrelated aims of comparative analysis, which would attract wide support from those working in the field.[2] In the first place comparison can produce a richer and more comprehensive *description* of foreign policy phenomena, by enabling the analyst to draw a more detailed and complete picture of events, processes and trends. Thus a description of British foreign policy in the 1980s can gain considerably from comparison with those of other West European countries faced with analogous problems. Second, comparison can provide insights into *correlation* or *causation*, going beyond description of *what* is the case to suggest *why* it is the case. The study of a range of comparable events or processes can reveal similarities or differences which help to test assumptions about associations between events or the causes of events. Comparison might thus suggest that dictatorships or military regimes tend to produce a particular style of foreign policy behaviour, distinct from that of liberal democracies.

Third, comparison may give grounds for *prediction*, by suggesting that in certain conditions certain patterns of foreign policy behaviour are likely to emerge. Despite the obvious difficulties of predicting any form of human behaviour, both the scholar and the practitioner find the need to form more or less well-founded expectations about what *will* happen in foreign policy – for example, the expectation that internal instability or civil unrest will affect the ability of policy-makers to function normally, or (more ambitiously) that the instability or unrest will have certain specific effects. Finally comparison can also be used as the basis for *prescription*, going beyond what is or might be the case to say what *ought* to be the case. The study of international relations has always had a strong prescriptive element, either because of its association with processes which arouse strong moral or ethical sentiments (such as peace and war) or because of the analysts' desire to influence the policy-makers directly, and foreign policy analysis is certainly no exception to this rule. For example, it is a very short step from the statement that democracies do produce certain types of policy style to the assertion that they ought to produce either that style or another, as several of the more dramatic debates about American foreign policies have shown. Equally the debate over British membership of the European Community, both before and after it was achieved in 1973, rested on the assumption not only that Britain was a 'European' state comparable to several others but also that 'Europeanism' ought to be a major goal of foreign policy. Much of the argument over 'rationality' in foreign policy decision-making also rests on a normative assumption that such a standard not only should but ought to be achieved.

Comparative approaches to foreign policy analysis thus rest on broad foundations which are shared with other social sciences. With those social sciences they also share great diversity of method. At a superficial level, it appears that there is extreme variation, amounting almost to anarchy, in the methods and techniques deployed by writers on comparative foreign policy. Historical analysis sits uncomfortably alongside behavioural investigation, while quantitative methods are ranged against qualitative or intuitive judgments. In this, foreign policy analysis shares the eclecticism and often sharp debates that have characterized the study of international relations more generally. At a more fundamental level, whatever the methods or techniques adopted, comparative approaches to foreign policy have a good deal in common. What is being compared in the vast majority of foreign policy studies, is precisely that relationship between the political unit and the conditions in which it operates that was noted at the beginning of the chapter. Accepting the basic concept of the foreign policy system put forward in Chapter 2, it becomes clear that there are three elements to the unit/conditions relationship; the qualities of political units and their characteristic processes, the conditions which produce demands upon them, and the responses which are produced by the interaction of the first two elements. These elements are the same irrespective of the range of units being compared or of the range of conditions in which they are compared. Thus a study of American foreign policy since 1945 (that is, of a single unit under changing conditions) is comparative; so is a study of Third World countries and their relations with the USA (a wide range of units in a specific context); and so is a study of Arab oil states with Washington (a restricted range of states with a restricted context). The relationship between unit and conditions, with its implications for policy responses, is thus a consistent and central concern.[3]

In the remainder of this chapter the emphasis is on three interrelated aspects of the relationship between foreign policy and the conditions in which it is made. First the focus is on the *problems* faced by policy-makers, and the ways in which these can be compared. Second, the analysis switches to the *processes* by which the problems are dealt with, and the ways in which these can vary according to circumstances. Finally the chapter explores the ways in which foreign policies can be subjected to comparative evaluation in terms of their *performance* against explicit criteria.

COMPARING FOREIGN POLICY PROBLEMS

Foreign policy analysts have long assumed that part of the 'foreign policy problem' reflects the kind of world within which foreign policies are pursued. As a result, many of the central writings in the field have focused their attention on the conditions within which the foreign policy system operates and produces action. Two particular foci of attention can be identified here: first the 'decision-making/systemic' dimension, and second, the 'realist-/pluralist' dimension. In the first case the contrast is between those analysts who have placed great emphasis on the ways in which conditions are perceived and defined by policy-makers, and those who have taken a broader view by focusing on the adaptation of national societies to a changing global environment.[4] As noted already, both of these approaches are inherently comparative, whatever their other differences. In the second case the distinction is between those who define foreign policy as the sole preserve of states and their governments and the problems as those emerging from a competitive state system, and those who define the field much more broadly to include the effects of a variety of actors and issues.[5] Again the comparative nature of the approaches is a central feature: the fact that they define the world in different ways does not mean that the responses of governments to it through foreign policy are any less central or interesting.

The 'foreign policy problem' can thus be defined in a number of different ways at the level of academic debate, but it remains remarkably constant at the level of substance. Broadly construed it concerns the set of constraints and stimuli faced by a foreign policy system, and extends to the system's ability to recognize and respond to the situations with which it is faced. As such, it can be used as the basis for a variety of comparative analyses, both those that focus on the problems faced by different national systems and those that stress the changing demands and opportunities faced by a single system. Central to these analyses is the proposition that while all foreign policy systems are faced by some common problems, each system confronts them in a unique form and responds to them in a unique way. The next task of this chapter is to identify and explore the major dimensions of the 'foreign policy problem', before proceeding to look at the ways in which they are faced and dealt with by foreign policy systems. In doing this, the chapter focuses on six dimensions: (i) size, status and involvement; (ii) economic and social development; (iii) internal political order; (iv) ideological orientation; (v) organizational networks; and (vi) international change. Individually each dimension encompasses a major area of concern in the literature of comparative foreign policy analysis, while collectively the six contribute to a sophisticated 'profile' of the foreign policy problems facing a given system and allow comparisons to be made with other systems.[6]

Size, Status and Involvement

Both analysts and practitioners have been consistently concerned with explaining the problems created by differences between states in terms of size, status and involvement. Traditional 'power politics' approaches would sum up these problems in the notion of an international hierarchy, in which the constraints and stimuli experienced by those at the top of the 'league table' are very different from those felt at the bottom. Attempts to construct an international hierarchy, though, reveal that 'size' is a multi-dimensional property, depending on much more than a simple measurement of population, territory, resources or gross national product.[7] The 'size' problem relates to that of status: clearly some states are accorded a higher status than others, not simply as a reflection of their raw strength but also as a result of their standing in the international system, the expectations generated and the roles they are asked to fulfil. To be a 'superpower' is thus not simply an expression of one-sided dominance, since it also encompasses a cluster of potent expectations and role conceptions which can constrain as well as empower.[8] Equally the position of a 'small' but highly regarded state, such as the Netherlands or Switzerland, can defy its position in the crude international hierarchy of strength and create unexpected openings for its policy-makers. The third element of the problem is that of involvement, which is far more than simply a measure of quantity. A state with many international involvements will face distinctive foreign policy problems, to be sure, and these can usefully be compared with the restricted range of involvements surrounding other foreign policy systems. The scope of involvement is thus important, but so also are the direction and the intensity of involvement, since it is these qualities which combine to create problems of choice and priorities for all systems. A 'small' state with limited contacts in the international arena may have no less of a problem in relation to its specific needs and resources than a major power with widely dispersed areas of concern entailing major commitments and demands.

Economic and Social Development

The wealth and sophistication of national societies have always been a significant element in the study of foreign policies, and the competition for markets or resources has been a major focus of foreign policy activity for centuries. During the 1950s and 1960s, however, new dimensions were added to the existing concern with economic and social development. A key factor here was the rapid emergence of new states after the collapse of the great colonial empires, which underlined (although it did not create) the disparities of wealth and resources in the world arena. Another influence – and one which became especially important in the 1970s and 1980s – was the growth of global interdependence, both between the rich countries of the 'north' and between them and the poor 'south'. Here again, though, the picture in terms of foreign policy problems is not one-dimensional. Clearly it is possible to argue that rich countries with highly developed institutional structures face fundamentally different problems from those with new and fragile economic and social orders, and that they have greater resources with which to overcome them. It is possible by combining these and other factors to construct two qualitatively different patterns or 'syndromes' of foreign policy problems: the 'modernized' and the 'unmodernized'. Such an argument is pursued by Edward Morse, for example, and can be used to compare the situations of a wide range of countries.[9] But between these two extremes there is clearly room for a large variety of 'mixes' involving those less developed countries that have modernized sectors or regions and those which although 'rich' have poor enclaves or backward industries. There is no doubt that the variations in economic vulnerability or social development between national societies are an important factor in foreign policy problems: studies of the differential impact of the oil crises during the 1970s, or of the impact of the international debt and banking problems during the 1980s, make this painfully clear.[10] As in the case of 'size, status and involvement', there is a subjective element as well as the raw facts of economic performance which must be considered, and this is vital to the choices and priorities pursued by policy-makers.

Internal Political Order

The role played by the internal political order in shaping foreign policy problems is clearly related to that of economic and social development. The contrast between a traditional view of foreign policy, in which 'politics stops at the water's edge', and a modernist view in which domestic needs and priorities interact with the international and transnational arenas, has been heightened by the changing substance of foreign policy itself, which has increasingly been affected by the interpenetration of the domestic and the international domains.[11] In terms of the foreign policy system, two features or dimensions of the internal political order are significant in shaping the foreign policy problem: first the 'openness' or 'closedness' of the regime, and second, the stability or instability of the political order itself. There has long been debate about the merits of comparing democratic and authoritarian regimes in the field of foreign policy, and the question not surprisingly remains an open one. More germane to the discussion here is the extent to which the foreign policy system is penetrated by the internal divisions or developments of the political system. If the foreign policy system reflects and is sensitive to the political aspirations of the society, then all well and good; but if it is closed to the debates and the shifts of political climate that can occur in even the most authoritarian of regimes, then it has a problem. This connects with the problem of stability and instability, since the foreign policy system is likely to be affected by the level of fragility or predictability in the governing arrangements of the society as a whole. If society is in chaos and the political order threatened, to what extent is this reflected in the foreign policy system? To put the point simply, the internal political order can be a source of significant problems for foreign policy-makers, and thus the comparative study of political systems in relation to foreign policy has an important role to play.[12]

Ideological Orientations

Ideology is a component of the foreign policy problem which cuts across and permeates many of the other elements. Not surprisingly the cold war years of the 1950s and early 1960s focused considerable attention on the potential role of ideology in the foreign policies of the two 'superpowers', while in the 1970s and the 1980s the focus has switched more to the Third World and the allegiances of governments there. The basic assumption and argument in this area has been that foreign policy systems implanted in societies where there is an established, explicit and comprehensive ideology, as opposed to those where there exists at most a set of unsystematized doctrines or preferences, will experience the foreign policy problem in distinctive ways. Two particular expressions of the general argument can be identified: first, from the point of view of the foreign policy system itself, and second, from the perspective of its relations with the outside world.

In the first case it appears that ideology can affect recruitment to the system and can thus determine who is, or will become, a policy-maker. Not only this, but it can shape the internal structure of the policy machine and can also mould the ways in which arguments are conducted within it. In other words the presence or absence of a formal ideology can be a significant feature of the context within which the foreign policy system operates, and can affect the style if not the substance of the policies produced. The substance of policy is also implicated in the second area of potential ideological influence: that of a country's pattern of international orientations and alignments. It is possible to argue that ideology conditions choices of friends and identification of adversaries – for instance in the Warsaw Pact and NATO – and it is also possible to compare patterns of activity in such areas as foreign aid or the recognition of governments by using ideology as a central variable. Whether this is a complete explanation is, of course, another matter, but it seems incontestable that ideology plays a role in the identification and handling of foreign policy problems.[13]

Organizational Networks

Much of what has been said in previous chapters points to the fact that organizational networks are important to foreign policy systems, and thus that they form a potential area of comparative analysis. Indeed one popular conception of the foreign policy system is that of a 'machine' demonstrating an integrity and coherence arising out of organizational patterns. As seen in Chapter 5, a great deal of the foreign policy analysis of the 1970s focused on organizational factors: one problem with this writing, though, was that it lacked some of the credentials of a truly comparative approach. To put it simply, it was argued that the literature of 'bureaucratic politics' could only draw upon the USA as a case study, and that the organizational forms of less developed or less 'open' societies did not lend themselves to a broader use of the approach. But such criticisms missed at least part of the point of comparison. While the focus was frequently on the USA, it was perfectly possible to compare within that focus and to explore the problems created by organizational processes or bureaucratic infighting in a number of different areas of policy. At the same time there is nothing inherent in organizational approaches which prevents cross-national comparison, and the 1980s have seen attention to cases in which the interesting thing was just how different they are from the American example – the closed societies of eastern Europe, or the less institutionalized countries of the Third World.[14]

It has also become apparent that organizational

networks within governments only represent one part of the problem. Increasingly governments find themselves conducting policies through international organizations of a bewildering variety, and this has direct effects on the definition of foreign policy problems. The countries of the European Community, for example, exist in an organizational environment unique in its density and comprehensiveness. It is a major element of any comparison between their foreign policies, and between their foreign policies and those of other countries, that this intense and continuous mutual organizational engagement exists. In western Europe, moreover, the density of transnational and transgovernmental links also constitutes a central feature of the policy environment. It is an open question whether these links provide advantages or impose constraints upon the policy-makers involved in them, but it is clear that the links themselves enter strongly into each of the foreign policy systems concerned.[15]

International Change

Foreign policy is made in a changing world and this automatically creates the possibility of comparisons between different types or phases of change as they affect the foreign policy problem. While change can be seen as forming part of the general background to any policy-making system, it can also throw up specific challenges to the policy-makers. How much of a problem this creates will depend, as Charles Hermann has pointed out, on the extent to which challenges are anticipated, the kinds of threats they pose and the urgency with which they are posed.[16] Clearly a consideration of such factors can provide the basis for comparison between different types of change and challenge. At one end of the spectrum appear the kinds of deliberative or almost 'routine' change which can be thoroughly anticipated and whose implications can be absorbed over an extended period. At the other end of the scale change can be surprising or even threatening and can demand a rapid response. One of the most taxing problems for policy-makers is that changes never occur singly, and thus there has to be a continuous process of 'practical comparison' between the policy-makers' expectations, the demands of many often contradictory chains of events and the possible implications, costs and benefits of many courses of action. Quite clearly these variations are of great significance. Since foreign policy can in part be defined as the attempt to reduce uncertainty in an uncertain world, there is an onus on policy-makers to develop accurate views of the distinction between significant and less significant change.[17]

COMPARING FOREIGN POLICY PROCESSES

Any discussion of the 'foreign policy problem' necessarily entails some consideration of foreign policy processes since, as already noted, a number of the problems confronting policy-makers arise from the relationship between their objectives or orientations and their capacity to respond to changing circumstances. Equally a consideration of the ways in which foreign policy processes might fruitfully be compared will inevitably draw upon the discussion in previous chapters dealing with the foreign policy system, with decision-making and implementation. The aim here is not to duplicate earlier arguments, rather it is to identify some crucial variations in the ways in which foreign policy processes perform key tasks. In this way, it will be possible to see processes of policy-making in relation both to the problems facing policy-makers and to the quality of the responses they produce. Two propositions are thus central to this part of the chapter: first that specific foreign policy problems will generate particular patterns in the foreign policy process; second, that certain types of process in themselves contribute to the problems faced by policy-makers by affecting their capacity for action and thus the overall performance of foreign policy systems.

Problems and Processes

Each of the six dimensions of the 'foreign policy problem' identified above can feed into the foreign policy process. Thus, for example, a state with extensive international involvement is likely to generate a complex foreign policy machine in order to service its commitments and to enhance its awareness of the issues in which it is entangled. Changes in the pattern of involvement are likely to lead to changes in the policy process as, for example, in the case of the loss of important overseas territories or the emergence of new issues. At the other end of the scale, a 'small' and less extensively involved state has no need for a large foreign policy apparatus, and the machine will focus on certain central areas of activity. In the same way there will be significant variations in foreign policy processes to reflect different social and economic priorities: the foreign policies of advanced industrial societies in western Europe are made in a socio-economic context very different from that of developing states in Latin America, and it is natural to assume that this will feed into the process of policy-making itself. Although some elements of the policy machine will undoubtedly be common to both groupings, others will express specific group needs and characteristics.

Another important source of variation in foreign policy processes is likely to be the political structure and ideological orientation of societies. To take only one example already mentioned, the 'openness' or 'closedness' of a regime is bound to affect the ways in which information is gathered and decisions are taken within the foreign policy system. There will be important variations and thus areas of comparison between the ways in which different foreign policy processes are open to changing events, to the needs of society and to the pressures of the world outside. Equally the foreign policy process can be subject to variations in the political stability of the regime in which it is implanted, as witness the virtual 'disappearance' of foreign policy at all but the verbal level in China during the Cultural Revolution of the late 1960s. The growth and consolidation of political stability, on the other hand, will enable the foreign policy process to proceed untrammelled by controversy or disruption. As noted earlier, the waxing or waning of ideological influences on foreign policy can affect recruitment into, and the operation of, the foreign policy system. Although direct and specific effects flowing from ideology are often hard to find, the more subtle shaping of leadership styles, the uses of information and the selection of courses of action, are other areas in which policy processes will reflect policy problems.

The operation of organizational networks can also have significant implications for the foreign policy process. Where bureaucracies are complex and large the energies of the policy-makers may be devoted simply to getting something through the system, without paying great attention to what is eventually produced. On the other hand, where bureaucracy is non-existent or fragmentary, foreign policy-making is more likely to reflect personalized decision-making styles, and to be based on a narrow range of skills and expertise. International or transnational networks have an increasing influence on national foreign policy processes. Indeed, for many governments these networks constitute an essential part of the policy environment, and they may penetrate the national policy process itself. Some governments, however, are more willing and better equipped to deal with this development than others, as studies of countries within the European Community or the Third World have revealed.[18]

Foreign policy processes face up to change and challenge in different ways. For all governments there are in effect two dimensions to this problem: the short-term and the long-term. Over the long term, turbulence within the policy environment can express itself in shifting alignments, in a changing international hierarchy or in the rise of novel demands. Foreign policy processes, willy-nilly, will be compelled to adjust to changing realities (although the policy-makers' capacity for resistance must not be underestimated): the adjustment can take the form of institutional restructuring, of shifts in perceptions and assumptions or of changes in the pattern of international involvement. Such incremental forms of adjustment and adaptation are not always possible in the short term, however. Indeed one of the essential features of crises is that they challenge not only the international order but also the operation of national foreign policy processes. As a result they can produce distinctive forms of policy-making characterized by restricted participation and debate and the by-passing of many decisional 'rules'. The coexistence of routine and innovation in foreign policy which is implied by such arguments provides another clear instance of the ways in which problems and processes are interrelated.[19]

Processes and Policy

From what has been said so far it is apparent that in comparing the workings of foreign policy processes, account must be taken of the problems they face. By comparing problems and relating them to the foreign policy system, estimates can be made of the capacity of the process to adjust or to accommodate different needs at different times. To take the argument further, it is necessary to focus on a further aspect of the foreign policy process; the ways in which different systems are able to perform the essential tasks related to adaptation or adjustment. These essential tasks or 'system functions' are three: first the generation of authority and legitimacy; second, the provision and interpretation of information; third, the mobilization of resources for the conduct of policy.

In discussing the problem of authority and legitimacy, the comparative analysis of foreign policy can draw upon a rich tradition in sociology and political science which has focused on the question of leadership. If foreign policy-makers are seen as the authoritative allocators of values and resources in relation to the external world, then variations in their authority are an important source of variations in foreign policy behaviour. Two interrelated aspects of the problem can be identified: first the sources of authority, and second, the style in which it is exercised. Max Weber the sociologist distinguished between three 'ideal types' of authority, the 'traditional', the 'rational —legal' and the 'charismatic'. More recently Henry Kissinger developed these types with specific reference to foreign policy in the late twentieth century, by identifying 'bureaucratic—pragmatic', 'charismatic' and 'revolutionary —ideological' sources of authority and legitimacy.[20] The first of these—'bureaucratic—pragmatic'—generates authority through an elaborate bureaucratic structure with a mass of rules and routines, designed to regularize and insulate the foreign policy process. On the other hand 'charismatic' authority depends upon personalized leadership and the qualities of the individual, and thus stands or falls with the leader concerned. Finally, 'revolutionary—ideological' authority derives from conformity with and preservation of the doctrines contained in a formal ideology, or a set of revolutionary traditions and values which help to identify the leaders and guide their policies.

The sources of authority thus shape its institutional forms, and it is clear from much of the discussion earlier in this chapter that this relationship can be crucial in understanding the comparative structures of foreign policy systems. But structure is not the only area to be affected by the sources of authority. As Kissinger was anxious to point out in his original writings on the subject, style can be an equally important barometer of the effects of variations or shifts in the bases of policy-making authority. Indeed Kissinger himself, through his association with the Nixon administrations in the USA between 1969 and 1974, came to have a decisive effect on the style of American foreign policy. Central to this impact was Kissinger's argument that the growth of bureaucracy and 'standard operating procedures' had cramped the style of successive presidents, and that in dealing with regimes whose authority rested on different foundations, the policy-makers needed to be free to create and innovate. Thus 'bureaucratic—pragmatic' authority was inefficient because it gave little freedom to the individual policy-maker, and because it handicapped the leadership in dealing with 'charismatic' or 'revolutionary–ideological' regimes. No clearer example could be found not only of the comparative evaluation of foreign policy processes but also of the link between the analytical and the operational elements of comparative foreign policy.

Two criticisms can be made of this rather neat illustration, though, and they are important. First, whatever the formal bases of authority in societies, it could be argued that this has relatively little impact on foreign policy. Because of its focus on national security and secrecy (at least in the traditional realist perspective), foreign policy everywhere is essentially 'undemocratic' and élitist. Therefore there may be less variation between apparently disparate regimes than would be expected at first glance. Second, it is apparent that whatever the general structure of authority and legitimacy in a given society there can be wide variations in the actual exercise of authority over foreign policy. The 'ideal types' are just that, and realistic comparisons must take account of a range of individual, institutional or political factors. A very good set of comparative examples in this area is furnished by precisely the variations between the influence and impact of successive American presidents that Kissinger identified.[21] To put this conclusion in the terms used earlier in this chapter, an account of authority and its exercise must be sensitive to the foreign policy problems faced by a given society as well as to its particular foreign policy apparatus.

As earlier chapters have suggested, a central task of any foreign policy process is the generation and interpretation of information. There are, however, likely to be important variations in the effectiveness with which this task is carried out. If information is the life-blood of policy-making, this is clearly because of its role in the definition of the foreign policy problem faced by a given system. As noted in Chapter 1, the absence of information is thus clearly a fundamental problem in itself; but problems can also be created by an excess of information, leading to overload and confusion. From this perspective it could be argued that the foreign policy processes of large complex systems are just as likely to suffer from problems as are those of small or less sophisticated systems. But according to Maurice East, the problems are different in quality. In a comparative study of large and small states, he concluded that one of the major variations between them lies in the capacities of their foreign policy processes to monitor their environments and to gather appropriate information about the challenges with which they are faced.[22] Whereas large states tend to have almost too much information about many issues, and thus find it difficult to isolate or decide about the key issues, small states lack the resources for such activities. The latter, therefore, have less 'margin for error' and are likely to demonstrate risky or erratic foreign policy behaviour. In reality the contrast is not as stark as this implies, since a variety of factors will mediate the impact of size: large states will develop ways of identifying the central issues, or bureaucracies will not function with the efficiency or predictability they are designed to achieve, while small states will specialize and develop expertise on the areas and issues that concern them most. None the less the uses and misuses of information in foreign policy processes are a key element in assessing their comparative performance.

A third task facing all foreign policy systems is that of mobilizing resources in support of policy choices. In many ways this task is related to issues of authority and information – indeed it could be said that authority and information are themselves key resources for any foreign policy system, and that variations in them are capable of enhancing or undermining its performance in fundamental ways. But at the level of policy implementation and the combination of material and intangible resources required there are certain very specific problems that can arise. In the first place there is the need to match resources with commitments: in other words the policy-makers' definition of the problems they face will (or should) be matched by the procurement and deployment of appropriate resources. Where involvements are extensive or demanding, or where resources are scarce and inflexible, then the capacity of the foreign policy process is likely to be taxed to the utmost, and this is a problem that can be faced by all states, no matter what their 'raw strength'. Thus in the late 1960s – and arguably in the 1980s as well – US policy-makers have found that competition between objectives can disable policy even where strength is immense. At the same time the careful concentration of attention and resources by weaker states can produce more effective policy, as in the case of a number of Arab oil producers in the 1970s. All systems, though, find that the allocation of resources is far from a simple mechanical process. Ideological commitments, domestic political and economic priorities, personal preferences and the inertia of existing commitments can all make their mark. In conditions of rapid change or uncertainty these influences can heighten the difficulties of foreign policy implementation, and thus the comparative evaluation of foreign policy performance must take them into account.[23]

COMPARING FOREIGN POLICY PERFORMANCE

As noted at the beginning of this chapter, an important function of comparison is to facilitate an accurate evaluation of policy performance. The social sciences in general, and foreign policy analysis in particular, have at their heart an attempt to assess the social world and either implicitly or explicitly to prescribe remedies for the problems that are thereby uncovered. Thus it is not surprising that many of the 'great debates' in foreign policy analysis have contained an inherent element of prescription. The aim has been not simply to derive more and better models of foreign policy, but also to improve the quality of policy itself, either in the ethical or in the empirical sense. American policy towards the USSR or the Third World, British policy towards western Europe or the Commonwealth, West German policy towards both East and West – are all examples of the ways in which the analysis and the evaluation of foreign policies have come together. Such debates are comparative in a highly significant way, since they entail the juxtaposition of policy against 'performance indicators' and against the results produced by alternatives pursued elsewhere or in different circumstances. In this final part of the chapter the emphasis is on the ways in which this kind of comparative evaluation can be conducted and related to both problems and processes in foreign policy.

The comparative evaluation of foreign policy performance implies some standards of quality, of 'success' or 'failure', of 'effectiveness' or 'ineffectiveness'. Because these qualities are often intangible or elusive they are not easy to conceptualize, and foreign policy-makers themselves are not accustomed to lay down explicit performance indicators for their activities. Where 'success' is apparently achieved, as in British membership of the European Community, it is often apparent that this only brings with it other problems, or masks problems that already exist. What seems to be required as a measure of quality is an approach that combines a number of elements and thus enables the balance of policy to be assessed. As Kenneth Waltz has argued:

> What is wanted in foreign policy is not a set of simple attributes but instead a nice balance of qualities: realism and imagination, flexibility and firmness, vigour and moderation, continuity of policy when policy is good and the ability to change direction when new international conditions make new departures desirable, adaptability of policy without destruction of its coherence or dependability.[24]

This makes it apparent not only that a multi-dimensional approach to the evaluation of foreign policies is necessary, but also that such evaluation has to be conducted in the light of the problems faced and the processes produced by different national societies. A number of analysts have attempted this kind of exercise, among them James Rosenau and Wolfram Hanrieder. Rosenau bases his argument on the assumption that for any society the essential standard for foreign policy effectiveness is the extent to which change in several coexisting arenas is kept within acceptable bounds. Hanrieder also argues that for many governments, the fundamental standard of 'success' in foreign policy is the extent to which the satisfaction of domestic and governmental needs can be combined with adaptation to external demands and the allocation of resources to competing activities.[25]

The notion of a 'balanced' foreign policy as a standard for comparative evaluation is thus well established, and can be seen on further examination to have a number of components. In the first place there is an acknowledged need for clarity of purpose, often in the face of confusing and demanding events. Second, there is the need for consistency in the integration of a number of strands to policy, which will entail the matching of objectives, targets and techniques. Alongside clarity and consistency, there is a need for continuity — that is, for the maintenance of a long-term or strategic perspective in the face of demands for short-term action or innovation. At the same time, and in line with Hanrieder's arguments, policy should be compatible with international and domestic conditions, and with the resources available to the country concerned. Finally, in the light of Rosenau's ideas, it is clearly important that policy should meet standards of adaptability: what is clear and consistent must not become rigid; what is acceptable in one area or at one time must not be allowed to ossify or to become a barrier to innovation. These five qualities — clarity, consistency, continuity, compatibility and adaptability — can be used as a series of yardsticks against which to judge the overall quality and the specific qualities of foreign policies on a comparative basis, either across time or across countries and issues. Equally important, the qualities can be viewed in relation to both the foreign policy problems and the foreign policy processes of a range of national societies.[26]

Foreign Policy Problems and Foreign Policy Performance

In assessing the performance of foreign policy systems, it is essential to relate the qualities of the policy produced to the problems faced by the system. Thus it is apparent that an important modifying factor in any country's achievement of a balanced policy is the range of international involvements and commitments pursued by the country. Large countries with extensive commitments will experience many competing demands, will need to deploy considerable resources to service their commitments and will experience many calls upon their attention and ability to innovate. The achievement of an appropriate balance in foreign policy is thus a matter of assiduous and detailed effort, and the costs of failure are likely to be considerable. Policy-makers will face problems of compatibility and adaptability simply because of the scale and the inherent inertia of many of their commitments, and policy itself may therefore be incremental rather than innovative or radical. On the other hand the problem for weak, small or dependent countries will be that of applying their limited attention and resources to a policy which might necessarily be unbalanced and apparently erratic. The point is that the notion of a balanced foreign policy enables comparative questions to be asked, not that similar answers are found.

A similar picture emerges from a study of other parts of the 'foreign policy problem' in relation to policy performance. A key role is played by problems of social and economic development: the fact that advanced industrial countries are entangled in networks of interdependence, and that they have major domestic welfare commitments, clearly imposes problems of priorities and balance between competing demands. But such demands are no less apparent for developing countries, which may be locked into dependency relations with the rich countries themselves and may have almost insurmountable problems of domestic economic provision.

Variations in the internal political order are likely to affect the balance of policy in a variety of ways. 'Open' societies may produce debates and pressures which are not experienced by 'closed' regimes, but they may as a result produce policies better founded on domestic consensus, even if the policies are more difficult to establish in the first place. Where regimes are unstable and chaotic, so may be the quality of policy in the international arena, but this does not automatically give the advantage to those with long traditions of stability and continuity, since they may be condemned to conservative incrementalism by precisely those forces. Ideology may set admirably clear objectives, but may produce distorted and inflexible policies if pursued to the exclusion of other factors. Organizational networks can provide additional resources and enhance the consistency or compatibility of policies, but not inevitably. At the same time they can impose constraints on the policy-makers and prevent them from adapting their priorities in the light of immediate or domestic needs. Finally the pervasiveness of change and uncertainty in foreign policy means that foreign policy-makers are faced with a central paradox in their pursuit of a balanced output. While they can frame their policies with the best of intentions, events may simply be outside their control, and the outcomes of policy may be far from those intended. Such a conclusion does not mean that the concept of 'balance' is irrelevant to the comparative evaluation of foreign policy performance. But it does mean that asking comparative questions about performance will produce a variety of answers reflecting the different foreign policy problems faced by a range of national societies.

Foreign Policy Processes and Foreign Policy Performance

It is clear from the last section that performance in foreign policy can only be assessed in the light of foreign policy problems. At the same time, account must be taken of the role played by foreign policy processes. It was argued earlier that foreign policy processes need to perform certain tasks – the generation of authority and legitimacy, the gathering and interpretation of information, the procurement and allocation of resources – and that there are significant variations in the ways in which different foreign policy systems approach and fulfil these needs. These variations are equally significant in accounting for the foreign policy performance of different systems.

The first 'system function' identified earlier was the generation of authority and legitimacy. This influences both the terms on which policy-makers hold and exercise their power and the ways in which that power is exercised. When it comes to the assessment of performance a number of consequences might follow. If authority is based on bureaucratic rules and routines, this can produce rigidities and barriers between different areas of policy, perhaps enhancing consistency and continuity at the expense of compatibility and adaptability. On the other hand charismatic authority generates strong, idiosyncratic leadership which may well enhance the clarity or adaptability of policy but may at the same time neglect the needs of consistency, continuity and compatibility. Authority based on ideological or revolutionary credentials may well produce a consistent view of the world, but it may stand in the way of adaptation to changing situations and emphasize continuity at the expense of compatibility. From this brief exploration of the issues, it appears that the quality of policy can be related not only to the ways in which policy-makers hold their authority, but also to the ways in which that authority is exercised.

Foreign policy systems also function as the guardians of the 'nerves of government': they have responsibility for the collection and interpretation of information, and the ways in which they do this can have material effects on the quality of policy they produce. Indeed the notion of a balanced foreign policy is inseparable from the correct definition of the context within which policy has to be pursued. Clarity of policy will reflect the ways in which information is gathered, alternatives are debated and choices are communicated to the outside world. Without the systematic use of information, each of the other desirable qualities of policy would be jeopardized: indeed in most foreign policies they *are* perpetually at risk because of the organizational, individual and ideological 'filters' which can operate to limit perceptions and the consideration of alternatives. The risks are intensified by a number of elements in the 'foreign policy problem' — size and capability, political order, the occurrence of challenge and crisis — which can bias the information available to and usable by the policy-makers.

When it comes to the mobilization of resources for the making and implementation of policy, it is again apparent that problems in this area can have further ramifications for the pursuit of quality in foreign policy. To put it simply, the resources necessary for the attainment of a balance may not be available, and those that are available may act to bias the policy options considered and selected by the policy-makers. This is important, since the notion of a balanced foreign policy assumes the ability to choose between different types of resources and to apply those chosen in an approriate way. The use of military force, for example, may well seem to impart an admirable clarity to policy, but it may jeopardize several of the other elements which are essential to a balanced strategy. Where resources are scarce and needs are pressing, the achievement of consistency or compatibilty between policy areas may have to be jettisoned. What this reveals is the role of policy-makers themselves as 'comparative analysts', since they have the perpetual task of relating diverse situations one to another and of comparing what might be desirable with what is possible in the light of available resources. As in the case of the other 'system functions', it reveals also the ways in which some kind of quality standards enhance the comparative analysis of foreign policy in general.

CONCLUSION

The starting point for this chapter was that the comparative analysis of foreign policy is an inevitable outcome of the way in which foreign policy analysis has grown in the context of the social sciences. Comparison is both necessary and useful, and is conducted by policy-makers as well as academics. At its most fundamental level, it consists of comparisons of political units and the conditions within which they operate — the 'political unit' in this case being the foreign policy system of a national society. The major

Figure 8.1 **Comparing Foreign Policies: Problems, Processes and Performance**

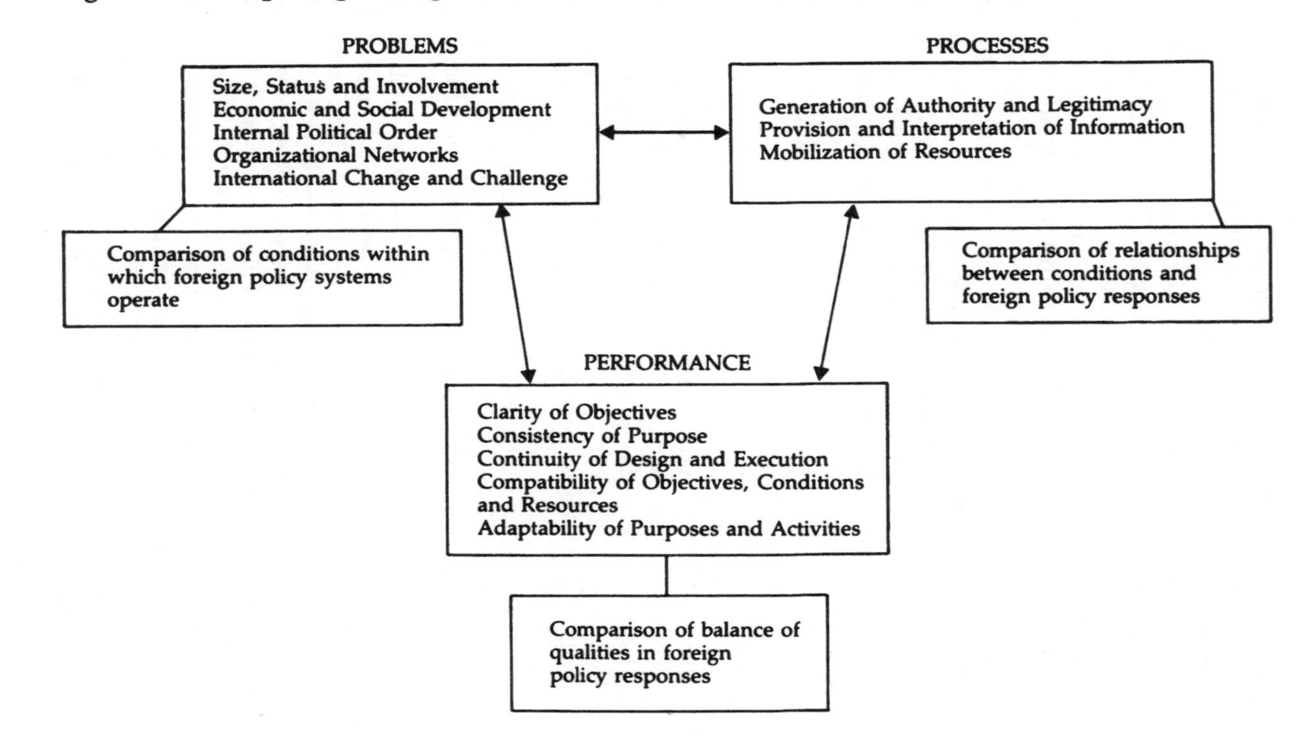

part of this chapter has conducted a systematic investigation of three major elements in this fundamental relationship, and has related them in turn to the ways in which comparison can be carried out. The elements are represented schematically in *Figure 8.1*, which acts as a summary of the argument which has been put forward. In essence, the conclusion is that foreign policy analysis inescapably involves the analyst in the comparative study of the 'foreign policy problem', of the foreign policy process, and of the ways that the problem and the process interact to produce distinct levels of foreign policy performance. Thus this chapter has presented a comparative framework which is intended to serve as a guide to a more effective understanding of particular case studies and issues.

NOTES

[1] Hanrieder, W., ed., *Comparative Foreign Policy: Theoretical Essays*, New York, McKay, 1971, Introduction, p. 2.
[2] Haas, M., 'On the Scope and Methods of Foreign Policy Studies' in McGowan, P., ed., *Sage International Yearbook of Foreign Policy Studies*, vol. 1, Beverley Hills, Calif., Sage, 1973, pp. 29–52.
[3] For a discussion of these and related issues, see Hermann, C., Kegley, C. and Rosenau, J. N., eds, *New Directions in the Study of Foreign Policy*, London, Allen & Unwin, 1987, Introduction and chs 2–4.
[4] For examples of the decision-making level of analysis, see Sprout, H. and M., *The Ecological Perspective on Human Affairs*, Princeton, NJ, Princeton University Press, 1965; Jervis, R., *Perception and Misperception in International Politics*, Princeton, NJ, Princeton University Press, 1976; Brecher, M. *et al.*, 'A Framework for the Research of Foreign Policy Behaviour', *Journal of Conflict Resolution*, 13, 1, March 1969, pp. 75–101. For examples of systemic analysis, see Rosenau, J. N., 'The External Environment as a Variable in Foreign Policy Analysis' in Rosenau, J. N. *et al.*, eds, *The Analysis of International Politics*, New York, Free Press; London, Collier-Macmillan, 1972, pp. 145–65; Rosenau, J. N. *The Study of Political Adaptation*, London, Pinter, 1981.

[5] These contrasts are explored in Smith, M., Little, R. and Shackleton, M., eds, *Perspectives on World Politics*, London, Croom Helm, 1981, esp. Parts 1 and 2. See also McKinlay, R. and Little, R., *Global Problems and World Order*, London, Pinter, 1986.
[6] For another study using several of these dimensions, see Jensen, L., *Explaining Foreign Policy*, Englewood Cliffs, Prentice-Hall, 1982.
[7] See, for example, Spiegel, S., *Dominance and Diversity: The International Hierarchy*, Boston, Little, Brown, 1972; Ray, J. L., *Global Politics*, New York, Houghton Mifflin, 1979.
[8] See, for example, Hoffman, S., *Gulliver's Troubles, or the Setting of American Foreign Policy*, Boston, Little, Brown, 1968; Bull, H., *The Anarchical Society: A Study of International Order*, London, Macmillan, 1977; Jonsson, C., *Superpower: Comparing American and Soviet Foreign Policy*, London, Pinter, 1984.
[9] Morse, E. L., *Modernization and the Transformation of International Relations*, New York, Free Press; London, Collier-Macmillan, 1976,esp. ch. 4.
[10] For a general review of these 'political economy' issues see Spero, J., *The Politics of International Economic Relations*, 3rd edn, London, Allen & Unwin, 1985.
[11] See Morse, E. L., op. cit.
[12] On these issues, see Farrell, R. B., 'Foreign Policies of Open and Closed Societies' in Farrell, R. B., ed., *Approaches to Comparative and International Politics*, Evanston, Ill., Northwestern University Press, 1966, pp. 167–208; Smith, M. and Williams, P., 'The Conduct of Foreign Policy in Democratic and Authoritarian Regimes', *Yearbook of World Affairs 1976*, pp. 205–23; Hagan, J., 'Regimes, Political Oppositions and the Comparative Analysis of Foreign Policy' in Hermann, C. *et al.*, op. cit. pp. 339–66; Jensen, L., op. cit. ch. 5.
[13] See, for example, Seton-Watson, H., 'The Impact of Ideology' in Porter, B., ed., *The Aberystwyth Papers: International Politics 1919–1969*, Oxford, Oxford University Press, 1972, pp. 211–37; Rosen, S. and Jones, W., *The Logic of International Relations*, 5th edn, Cambridge, Mass., Winthrop, 1985; Jensen, L., op. cit. ch. 4.
[14] See the discussion in Chapter 5, and also Adomeit, H. and Boardman, R., eds, *Foreign Policy-Making in Communist Countries*, Farnborough, Hants, Saxon House, 1979; Clapham, C.,

ed., *Foreign Policy-Making in Developing States*, Farnborough, Hants, Saxon House, 1979.

[15] On the general issue of international organization, see Jacobson, H. K. *et al.*, 'National Entanglements in International Governmental Organizations', *American Political Science Review*, 80, 1, March 1986, pp. 141–59; Doxey, M. 'International Organization in Foreign Policy Perspective', *Yearbook of World Affairs 1975*, pp. 173–95. On the impact of transnational and transgovernmental organizations, see Keohane, R. and Nye, J., *Power and Interdependence: World Politics in Transition*, Boston, Little, Brown, 1977; 'Transgovernmental Relations and International Organizations', *World Politics*, 27, 1, October 1974, pp. 39–62. On western Europe in particular, see Wallace, W. and Paterson, W., eds, *Foreign Policy-Making in Western Europe*, Aldershot, Saxon House, 1978; Hill, C., ed., *National Foreign Policies and European Political Cooperation*, London, Allen & Unwin, 1983.

[16] See Hermann, C., 'International Crisis as a Situational Variable' in Rosenau, J., ed., *International Politics and Foreign Policy*, 2nd edn, New York, Free Press; London, Collier-Macmillan, 1969, pp. 409–21.

[17] On this point see Smith, M., 'Significant Change and the Foreign Policy Response: Some Analytical and Operational Implications' in Buzan, B. and Jones, R. J. B., eds, *Change and the Study of International Relations: the Evaded Dimension*, London, Pinter, 1981, pp. 209–24; Hermann, C., 'Why New Foreign Policy Challenges Might Not be Met: Constraints on Detecting Problems and Setting Agendas' in Kegley, C. and McGowan, P., eds, *Challenges to America: United States Foreign Policy in the 1980s*, Beverley Hills and London, Sage, 1979, pp. 269–90.

[18] See Clapham, C., ed., op. cit.; and Wallace, W. and Paterson, W., eds, op. cit.

[19] See Hermann, C., 1969, op. cit.; and also Lovell, J. P., *The Challenge of American Foreign Policy: Purpose and Adaptation*, New York, Macmillan, 1985.

[20] Kissinger, H., 'Domestic Structure and Foreign Policy', *Daedalus*, 95, Spring 1966, pp. 503–29. For another perspective on leadership issues, which emphasizes variations in the impact of personalities, see Hermann, M., 'When Leader Personality Will Affect Foreign Policy: Some Propositions' in Rosenau, J., ed., *In Search of Global Patterns*, New York, Free Press; London, Collier-Macmillan, 1976, pp. 326–32.

[21] See Kissinger, H., op. cit.; and Brown, S., *The Faces of Power: Constancy and Change in American Foreign Policy From Truman to Reagan*, New York, Columbia University Press, 1983.
[22] East, M., 'Size and Foreign Policy Behaviour: a Test of Two Models', *World Politics*, 24, 4, July 1973, pp. 556–76.
[23] See Chapter 7 for a full account of the implementation perspective.
[24] Waltz, K., *Foreign Policy and Democratic Politics*, Boston, Little, Brown, 1967, p. 16.
[25] See Rosenau, J., 1981, op. cit.; Hanrieder, W., 'Compatibility and Consensus: a Proposal for the Conceptual Linkage of External and Internal Dimensions of Foreign Policy' in Hanrieder, W., ed., op. cit. pp. 242–64.
[26] For a full discussion of these ideas see Smith, M. and Williams, P., op. cit. They are discussed in relation to the problem of change in Smith, M., op. cit.

Index